From its flying-wing design, to its radar-deflecting stealth capabilities, to its nuclear bomb-delivering capacity, the B-2 is one awe-inspiring war machine. In *B-2 Spirit*, popular aviation author Steve Pace delivers a razor's-edge portrait of this sinister-looking plane's daring design, development, and deployment.

You'll read the exciting story of how Northrop Grumman developed this great leap forward in military aviation technology, a startling advance even over its own thrillingly foresighted B-49. You'll be there as the B-2, code-named "Project Senior Ice"...

- Asserts itself as the most dominant bomber in military aviation history
- Emerges triumphant from a phalanx of flying wing designs
- Undergoes intensive flight testing that brought this revolutionary warcraft into operation in just eight years
- Receives design modifications for an 80-bomb or 40-bomb capacity, and conversion to a 16-bomb nuclear platform in less than an hour
- Takes to the skies, ready for wartime operation in campaigns such as Kosovo

With more photos than have ever been available in the public domain, including an eight-page color-photo insert, *B-2 Spirit* brings you closer to the B-2 than civilians have previously been allowed to venture.

Packed with details on this exciting plane's history and more information on its structures and systems than has ever been published in a single unclassified source, Steve Pace's *B-2 Spirit* is the next best thing to flying the most advanced bomber in the world.

B-2 SPIRIT

B-2 SPIRIT

The Most Capable War Machine on the Planet

Steve Pace

McGraw-Hill

New York   San Francisco   Washington, D.C.   Auckland   Bogotá
Caracas   Lisbon   London   Madrid   Mexico City   Milan
Montreal   New Delhi   San Juan   Singapore
Sydney   Tokyo   Toronto

Library of Congress Cataloging-in-Publication Data

Pace, Steve.
    B-2 Spirit : the most capable war machine on the planet /
Steve Pace.
        p.   cm.
    Includes index
    ISBN 0-07-134433-0
    1. B-2 bomber.   I. Title.
UB1242.B6P315   1999
623.7'463—dc21   99-29342
                                                    CIP

McGraw-Hill

*A Division of The **McGraw·Hill** Companies*

ISBN 0-07-134434-9

The sponsoring editor for this book was Shelley Carr, the editing supervisor was Frank Kotowski, Jr., and the production supervisor was Sherri Souffrance.

It was set in Utopia at North Market Street Graphics.

Printed and bound by Quebecor/Kingsport.

McGraw-Hill books are available at special quantity discounts to use as premiums and sales promotions, or for use in corporate training programs. For more information, please write to the Director of Special Sales, McGraw-Hill, 11 West 19th Street, New York, NY 10011. Or contact your local bookstore.

 This book is printed on recycled, acid-free paper containing a minimum of 50% recycled, de-inked fiber.

In memory of John Knudson Northrop,
1895–1981

CONTENTS

The McGraw-Hill Companies is pleased to present the **Walter J. Boyne Military Aircraft Series.** The series will feature comprehensive coverage, in words and photos, of the most important military aircraft of our time.

Profiles of aircraft critical to defense superiority in World War II, Korea, Vietnam, the Cold War, the Gulf Wars, and future theaters detail the technology, engineering, design, missions, and people that give these aircraft their edge. Their origins, the competitions between manufacturers, the glitches and failures, and type modifications are presented along with performance data, specifications, and inside stories.

To ensure that quality standards set for this series are met volume after volume, McGraw-Hill is immensely pleased to have Walter J. Boyne on board. In addition to his overall supervision of the series, Walter is contributing a Foreword to each volume that provides the scope and dimension of the featured aircraft.

Walter was selected as editor because of his international preeminence in the field of military aviation and particularly in aviation history. His consuming, lifelong interest in aerospace subjects is combined with an amazing memory for facts and a passion for research. His knowledge of the subject is enhanced by his personal acquaintance with many of the great pilots, designers, and business managers of the industry.

As a Command Pilot in the United States Air Force, Colonel Boyne flew more than 5000 hours in a score of different military and civil aircraft. After his retirement from the Air Force in 1974, he joined the Smithsonian Institution's National Air & Space Museum, where he became Acting Director in 1981 and Director in 1986. Among his accomplishments at the Museum were the conversion of Silver Hill from total disarray to the popular and well-maintained Paul Garber Facility, and the founding of the very successful *Air&Space/ Smithsonian* magazine. He was also responsible for the creation of NASM's large, glass-enclosed restaurant facility. After obtaining permission to install IMAX cameras on the Space Shuttle, he supervised the production of two IMAX films. In 1985, he began the formal process that will lead ultimately to the creation of a NASM restoration facility at Dulles Airport in Virginia.

Boyne's professional writing career began in 1962; since that time he has written more than 500 articles and 28 books, primarily on aviation subjects. He is one of the few authors to have had both fiction and nonfiction books on *The New York Times* best seller lists. His books include four novels, two books on the Gulf War, one book on art, and one on automobiles. His books have been published in Canada, Czechoslovakia, England, Germany, Italy, Japan, and Poland. Several have been made into documentary videos, with Boyne acting as host and narrator.

Boyne has acted as consultant to dozens of museums around the world. His clients also include aerospace firms, publishing houses, and television companies. Widely recognized as an expert on aviation and military subjects, he is frequently interviewed on major broadcast and cable networks, and is often asked by publishers to review manuscripts and recommend for or against publication.

Colonel Boyne will bring his expertise to bear on this series of books by selecting authors and titles, and working closely with the authors during the writing process. He will review completed manuscripts for content, context, and accuracy. His desire is to present well-written, accurate books that will come to be regarded as definitive in their field.

ACKNOWLEDGMENTS

This reference could not have been produced without the very kind assistance provided by the following individuals: Elaine Anderson, Jo Anne Davis, Mike Lombardi, Mike Tull, Dick Ziegler, The Boeing Company; Major Linda Hutchins, Aeronautical Systems Center Public Affairs; Captain Bruce Sprecher, Senior Airman Polly Gates, 509th Bomb Wing Public Affairs; Shirley Darrow, Mike Greywitt, Ed Smith, Military Aircraft Systems Division, Northrop Grumman Corporation; Dennis Shoffner, Air Force Flight Test Center Public Affairs; Kirsten Tedesco, Scott Thompson, Pima Air and Space Museum; Captain Tess Taft, B-2 System Program Office Public Affairs; Chris Wamsley, Erik Simonsen, Boeing North American; Denny Lombard, Lockheed Martin Skunk Works; Douglas Bullard, Nurflugel; Tony Landis; Fred Johnsen, Ray Puffer, Air Force Flight Test Center History Office; Shelley Carr, Walter Boyne, Frank Kotowski, Jr., Mary Haramis, The McGraw-Hill Companies.

The concept of stealthy aircraft has been with us since the First World War. Then various types of camouflage were tried, engines were muffled, and the Germans even replaced the fabric covering of the fuselage of the twin-engine Linke-Hofman R I bomber with Cellon, a transparent-celluloid material they felt would render it invisible. Almost everything had defects: the camouflage worked only at a distance and against certain backgrounds; the mufflers absorbed too much power from the engine; and the Cellon-covered aircraft glistened like a mirror, reflecting the sun.

The efforts became a little more sophisticated over time, just as the demands became greater. By World War II, fairly effective paint schemes had been developed. Birds-egg blues were used to mask the passage of high altitude aircraft. (The paint could not conceal contrails, however, a problem that persisted for another generation.) Deep blacks were universally and successfully used on aircraft operating at night, along with flame-dampeners for the exhausts. Special camouflages were created for winter and for desert conditions.

There were even some interesting experiments using lights mounted on aircraft to diminish their visibility by mimicking the background light. The idea was theoretically successful, but impractical in practice.

Dampening sound became almost irrelevant with the advent of radar. Scientists turned tentatively to find ways of masking radar returns with special paints and various types of radar-absorbent material (RAM), but without great success. During the postwar world, research advanced the art of radar far more rapidly than it did the art of radar avoidance, and massive radar networks spread up as fences dividing the two opposing camps in the Cold War.

It was noted in passing that some aircraft, such as the Northrop YB-49, had naturally low radar signatures, but not much advantage was taken of the idea. It had been hoped that the Lockheed U-2 would be stealthy, but this was not the case. However, the Lockheed A-12/SR-71 series of aircraft was the first operational aircraft to have some stealth characteristics included in the design. The Radar Cross Section (RCS) was reduced, and RAM material was included in its construction.

But stealth did not become a discipline of overwhelming importance until there were breakthrough discoveries at first Lockheed and then Northrop. The Lockheed formula for success was derived from a perceptive interpretation by Denys Overholser of an obscure 1966 Russian technical paper by Pyotr Ufimtsev. Overholser created a computer program named ECHO I which has been called the "Rosetta Stone" of stealth, for it unlocked the secrets by which an aircraft's shape could be made to deflect radar signals. The Lockheed

Skunk Works used these studies as a basis for creating first the Have Blue prototypes and then the F-117A Stealth Fighter.

Northrop's approach to stealth was lead by John Cashen, Irving Waaland, and John Patierno, among others, using the most advanced Cray supercomputers. By a kindly providence, the Northrop approach led them where tradition might have: to the flying wing as an idealized shape for the next generation of stealth aircraft, the Advanced Technology Bomber.

The term Advanced Technology Bomber is sometimes understood to refer primarily to stealth. Nothing could be further from the truth, for the ATB, as delivered by the Northrop Grumman B-2, features advances in materials, manufacture, aerodynamics, armament, and operational concept in addition to advances in stealth technology.

It also embodies the expression of national division and indecision on the basic role the United States should play as the sole remaining superpower. Since the fall of the Soviet Union, the United States has, under different administrations, increasingly assumed the role of peacekeeper and policeman to the world. At the same time, defense spending has been slashed (more than 40 percent since the Persian Gulf War). It should be noted that the slashes to the defense budget have come at the time of the nation's greatest prosperity, and the percent of the Gross Domestic Product spent on defense is at its lowest point since before World War II.

More important, the force structure has been drawn down, research and development funds reduced, and spending on "big-ticket" items such as the B-2 are bitterly opposed as being unnecessary and wasteful. In the past, bombers had been produced in great quantity, anticipating normal attrition to accidents in peacetime, and, of course, a higher rate during wartime. Thus, in the postwar period, the USAF purchased 2,032 Boeing B-47s, 744 Boeing B-52s, and 100 Rockwell International B-1Bs. The initial planning for the B-2 called for the purchase of 132 aircraft. Rising costs and the perception of a diminished threat have reduced this to a total force of only 21 B-2s, deployed in two squadrons.

One hopes and prays that there will be no attrition ever in the B-2 force, but that is unlikely. The loss of just one aircraft will reflect an almost five percent reduction in the force. It also has to be recognized that, as the fleet gains maturity, there will be first an increase in serviceability, followed by an inevitable decline as systems get older and spare parts become less available. While initial maintainability goals are high, it would be reasonable to assume that the B-2 fleet will have as many as five or more aircraft out of service at any one time. This means that the reduction in budgets will result in a fleet of only 10 to 15 first-line bombers to defend the richest country in the world. (There will still be a force of 20-year-old B-1Bs and 50-year-old B-52s to rely on.)

We should ask ourselves this question: As the richest nation in the world, as the sole superpower, as the self-appointed world's policeman, is this enough to do the job?

Unfortunately, the implications of the high cost of the B-2 goes far beyond its own operational career. With all research and development costs now allocated to just 21 aircraft, the unit cost has risen drastically, to the point that B-2 opponents now call each aircraft—not just the program—a "two billion dollar blunder." The degree of bitter opposition, too, and resentment of, the B-2 has reached a point that any discussion of a follow-on manned bomber is moot. Military planners feel that an advanced manned bomber is necessary, but the subject is so fraught with political risk that it is not openly discussed.

There is one major hope for a future bomber, and that is if the performance of the B-2, over the next 10 years, lives up to its promise. If, as Steve Pace's immensely detailed narrative reveals, the B-2 proves to be as effective and efficient as is claimed, then there may yet be another manned bomber.

—Walter J. Boyne

The Northrop Grumman B-2A Spirit is a milestone in bomber history, one that combines remarkable technological advances with an historic flying wing configuration. The B-2 was called into being as a result of changing political, economic, and war-making requirements. During the long years of the Cold War, the concept of mutually assured destruction by massive nuclear forces maintained a tenuous peace. Huge bomber and missiles forces were required to deter the powerful Soviet Union from a first strike. With the decline of the Soviet Union and the lessening of the requirement for massive nuclear retaliation, it became necessary to create a bomber that could elude enemy radar defenses and surgically strike selected targets. In the past, increased speed and altitude capabilities had been the goal for advancing bomber survivability. The B-2A's performance is not significantly better than the veteran Boeing B-52 in terms of speed and altitude. It is, however, much longer ranged, and is endowed with the modern *sine qua non* of bomber requirements: stealth.

Stealth characteristics require special shapes, materials, and methods of construction. The first operational stealth "fighter" (in reality, an attack bomber), the Lockheed F-117A, used sharply faceted plates as the principal means of radar avoidance. (Industry mergers have confounded designations: the stealth fighter is now identified as a Lockheed Martin F-117A, and what was originally a Northrop B-2A is now a Northrop Grumman B-2A.) The designers of B-2A approached the problem differently, using smooth shapes to achieve the same goal of reflecting radar signals away from their source.

Economics also had its effect upon the B-2A program, which was successively reduced from its original 132 plane goal to its final 21 aircraft procurement. The decline in the perceived threat and the desire to reduce military spending have resulted in the creation of the most capable and the most expensive bomber in history.

Despite its relatively small numbers, the B-2A has added immeasurably to the strength of the United States Air Force's Air Combat Command. Its inherent ability to operate without the large fleet of tankers and electronic warfare aircraft required by older bombers such as the B-52 makes it most effective for dealing with the range of threats anticipated today.

Some of the most notable bombers in American history have made their mark without ever dropping a bomb. A short list would include the Martin B-10, the Convair B-36, and the Boeing B-47. It was hoped that a similar fate would have befallen the B-2, that it might have a long and useful career, never having to be used in combat. But recent events in the former Republic of Yugoslavia have dashed these hopes.

In any case, whether the B-2 is used long and often in combat, or flies in a conflict free world, it is a landmark design both because of its extraordinary stealth technology and the unprecedented methods used in its creation. Developed under extreme conditions of security by a remarkable industrial consortium, this technology has already generated many spin-offs that will affect aircraft and missile design for the future.

—STEVE PACE

B-2 SPIRIT

The Spirit of Jack Northrop

"It [the stealth bomber] doesn't have any wings. It is one."

—AN ANONYMOUS NORTHROP B-2 DIVISION EMPLOYEE, LATE 1987

The concept of a flying wing is steeped in nature and in history. The *Zanonia macrocarpa* seed of Java flies beautifully from its vine to earth, demonstrating an inherent stability as it was carried by the wind that fostered its survival. The first man-made use of the shape might be found in the boomerang of Australia's Aborigine warriors. They used the throwing device for sport and war.

The first flying wing aircraft appeared as long ago as May 21, 1870, when Richard Harte of Kensington, in the County of Middlesex, Great Britain, petitioned Her Majesty to grant Her Royal Letters Patent for an invention for "Improvements in Means and Apparatus for Effecting Aerial Locomotion." This patent specification (No. 1469 of the year 1870) describes a tailless monoplane having some of the features as follows: (1) Flaplike controllers serving in modern fashion as elevators and ailerons (i.e., simultaneously and differentially controlled); (2) Neutralization of the torque reaction of the rotating airscrew [propeller] by differential deflection of controller flaps; (3) Employment of ailerons for the purpose of circling flight (e.g., as generators of yawing [movement about the vertical axis] moments), in place of any vertical rudder surfaces; (4) Longitudinal [control over the rolling movement of an aircraft] trim effected by shifting the center of gravity; and (5) Provision for longitudinal balance during take-off and for neutralizing the airscrew [propeller] thrust moment. Harte, though his work never became more than a patent, may be called the inventor of the tailless airplane, or the flying wing airplane, and features similar to his patent are employed by today's B-2 flying wing bomber.

Many other aeronautical pioneers created their own versions of flying wing aircraft, some with great success. These include Alphonse Penaud, Clement Ader, Igo Etrich, John Dunne, Hugo Junkers, Alexander Lippisch, and the Horten brothers, Walter and Reimar. The Hortens were perhaps the most successful of this group, for they created many designs ranging from simple gliders to advanced jet fighters that would have seen service in World War II had it lasted another year.

But, of all the many great flying wing pioneers, the most accomplished was the American, John Knudsen "Jack" Northrop.

Jack Northrop: King of the Flying Wing

John K. Northrop was born in Newark, New Jersey, on November 10, 1895. Today, more than 100 years later, Mr. Northrop is widely recognized as one of the world's most inventive and prolific aircraft designers. He designed the famous wooden Lockheed Vegas and began the manufacture of sophisticated metal aircraft such as the Northrop Alpha and Gamma.

He is best known, however, for his numerous aircraft designs based on semi-flying wing and pure all-flying wing configurations. In these designs, the aircraft has no fuselage and limited or no tail group assemblies. The purpose of the flying wing concept was to reduce the aircraft's parasite drag and weight, and thus increase its lift and range.

Northrop believed his flying wings would fly farther, faster, and higher than conventional aircraft. In many respects his ideas were in advance of an essential component that would guarantee stability: the modern computer. As it happened, his flying wing designs would not reach operational use. It was not until the first public appearance of the first B-2 in November 1988 that it became apparent how far in advance his thinking really was.

As America's chief advocate for flying wing aircraft, Jack Northrop tried to design, develop, and produce viable fighter and bomber aircraft primarily for the U.S. military. Unfortunately, Northrop died on February 18, 1981, not long after he had been secretly briefed on his former firm's plan to build what was then called the advanced technology bomber, or ATB. He was extremely pleased with the ATB's design, for it featured an all-flying wing configuration. Afterwards, according to John Cashen—Northrop's "Dr. Stealth"—Northrop was heard to say: "Now I know why God has kept me alive for the last 25 years."

Wings, Wings, and More Wings

Jack Northrop converses with famed test pilot Eddie Bellande. Simply called the 1929 Flying Wing (X-216H), this was Northrop's first venture into building an aircraft that featured more wing area than tailplane area. Although it had twin booms, a horizontal tail with elevators, and two vertical tails with rudders, it was referred to as a bona fide semi-flying wing. It is shown here in its final configuration as a pusher at Northrop's Hawthorne, California, facility in the summer of 1929. Its first flight occurred on September 26, 1929. *(The Boeing Company Archives)*

Jack Northrop created his first flying wing-like aircraft in the very late 1920s. Simply referred to as the 1929 Flying Wing, it was a single-engine aircraft powered by a 90-hp piston engine turning a two-bladed propeller. Originally built as a tractor (propeller in front), his little side-by-side two-seater performed well, but not well enough to suit Northrop. It was later modified to a pusher (propeller in back), and its testing resumed. It was not a true flying wing aircraft—it had twin booms, a horizontal stabilizer, and two vertical stabilizers—but it gave Northrop valuable experience.

Northrop's goal was to create a pure all-flying wing with no tail surfaces whatsoever. He believed that an all-flying wing aircraft would weigh 10 percent less than conventional aircraft carrying the same payload. All other things being even, a flying wing would have less drag and would fly farther with the same fuel capacity, cruising speed, and cruising altitude than a conventional aircraft.

With limited military funding and using in-house resources, Northrop and the company he founded went on to create a number of flying wing aircraft. These include the N-1M, N-9M, JB-1 and JB-10; XP-56, MX-324 and MX-334; XP-79 and XP-79B; XB-35 and YB-35; and the YB-49 and YRB-49A.

The 1929 Flying Wing was originally built as a tractor (propeller in front), as shown here. Flight tests demonstrated its better performance as a pusher. *(AFFTC/HO)*

Jack Northrop was a leader in the successful design of extremely strong and light aircraft structures. Northrop is shown standing next to a test beam that was built using his construction method, with some 500 bricks sitting on top of the beam; it is readily apparent just how strong one of his relatively thin and narrow structures was. The beam, which actually is composed of metal boxes or "cells," simulates a wing undergoing a simple test of its strength. *(The Boeing Company Archives)*

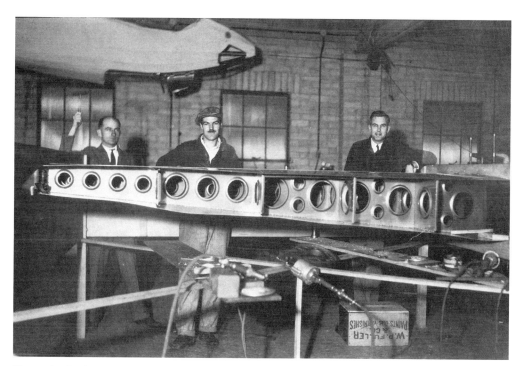

Shown is the inside of the 1929 Flying Wing looking rearward at the spar (with weight-lightening holes), which forms one side of the grid in "multicellular" construction. The aircraft, built on plywood frames, served as its own mock-up. *(The Boeing Company Archives)*

The N-1M

In the late 1930s and early 1940s, Northrop obtained military funding to further his dream. Under the guise of N-1M (Northrop model number one, mock-up), Northrop was officially authorized to create what became an all-flying wing aircraft.

The N-1M (NX-28311) made its first flight at Muroc Dry Lake (now Rogers Dry Lake) on July 3, 1940. The unique aircraft had no horizontal or vertical tails, and during some 200 test flights, it demonstrated excellent flying characteristics. The N-1M was tested with both downturned and straight wing tips. The latter configuration proved to be the most acceptable for stability and control.

The N-9M

Northrop was contracted to build four N-9M aircraft to serve as subscale prototypes for the U.S. Army Air Forces (formerly U.S. Army Air Corps) upcoming XB-35 flying wing bomber program under project MX-140. The first two N-9Ms—and a third designated N-9M-A—were powered by two 275-hp Menasco engines spinning pusher propellers. The fourth aircraft, designated N-9M-B, was powered by two 300-hp Franklin engines.

The first N-9M made its first flight on December 27, 1942, and after some 30 hours of flight-test activities, it crashed, killing its pilot, Max Constant. The remaining three N-9M aircraft, however, flew the remainder of their flight-test programs without mishap, clearing the way for Northrop to proceed on the controversial XB-35 Flying Wing Bomber program.

In the early 1940s, Northrop's company produced several N-9M semi-flying wing aircraft as subscale prototypes for Northrop's two XB-35 Flying Wing bombers. Much closer to a pure flying wing, the N-9M was quite successful. The first example is shown outside a makeshift hangar housing the second of two Northrop XP-56 "Black Bullet" prototypes. The hangar was located at what is now called North Base at Edwards AFB (then Muroc Army Air Field). The brand-new 1941 Chevrolet two-door post is noteworthy. *(AFFTC/HO)*

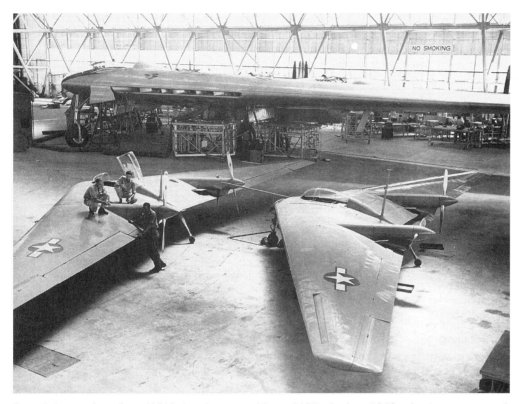

A much better view of two N-9Ms in a hangar at Muroc AAF in the late 1940s. As you can see, neither one of the N-9M aircraft have horizontal or vertical tailplanes. The aircraft in the background is one of the two Northrop XB-35 piston-powered Flying Wing bomber prototypes. *(AFFTC/HO)*

The first N-9M as it appeared just before its first flight. Following the relatively successful flight operations of its immediate predecessor aircraft—the Northrop N-1M—and the successful N-9M test hops, the way was cleared for Northrop's venture into larger flying wing aircraft. *(AFFTC/HO)*

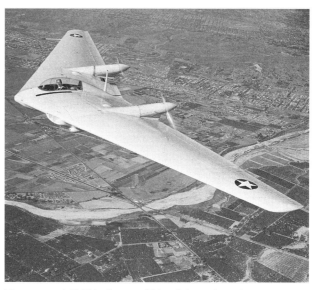

As it banks right, the first of four N-9M aircraft is shown as it appeared during its first flight at Muroc AAF. Shades of today's B-2 Spirit. *(AFFTC/HO)*

The second N-9M shows off its flying wing characteristics during a test hop. *(AFFTC/HO)*

The JB-1 and JB-10

Under USAAF Air Materiel Command (AMC) projects MX-543 and MX-544, Northrop created a pair of flying wing-like jet-powered bombs, the JB-1 "Bat" and JB-10 "Vampire Bat." In early 1940s Air Force jargon, the prefix *JB* meant "jet bomb." These so-called jet bomb aircraft were built to serve as unmanned flying bombs a la the German V-1 buzz bombs of World War II. (The *MX* prefix denotes "materiel, experimental.")

Northrop built a piloted single-engine JB-1 to serve as the prototype for the nonpiloted

Three of the four N-9Ms fly in a loose formation after the demise of N-9M number one. *(AFFTC/HO)*

Prior to the advent of the N-9M aircraft, Northrop tested two versions of its N-1M—one with drooped wing tips (shown) and one with straight wings. With a number of successful flight tests between these two N-1M versions, the way was cleared for the N-9M. *(AFFTC/HO)*

JB-1A production vehicles. The JB-1As carried a pair of 2,000-lb high-explosive (HE) warheads housed within two fairings, one on either side of its main body.

The success of the piloted JB-1 prototype led to the production of a number of nonpiloted JB-1As. The JB-1A's accomplishment opened the door for the larger and more destructive JB-10. The nonpiloted twin-engine JB-10 featured a single 3,700-lb HE warhead, and with its two engines, it featured improved altitude and speed capabilities over its JB-1 counterpart.

The XP-56

Two XP-56 aircraft were built as experimental pursuit (fighter) aircraft to the same Request for Data (R-40C) as the Convair XP-54 Swoose Goose (MX-12) and Curtiss XP-55 Ascender.

The original straight-wing N-1M as it appeared after its completion at Northrop's Hawthorne facility. Essentially, it was a subscale prototype for the proposed Northrop N-1, a twin-engine flying wing bomber. *(Northrop Grumman)*

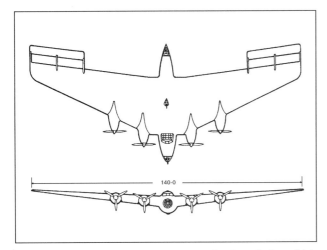

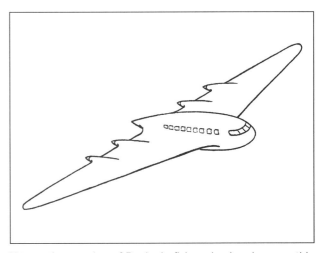

Jack Northrop worked a short time at Boeing, during which his dream of creating flying wing aircraft surfaced again. This long-range bomber version of a flying wing had a huge-for-the-time 140-ft wingspan and a pressurized cabin, and was to carry a crew of 11. *(The Boeing Company Archives)*

Yet another version of Boeing's flying wing bomber was this 4-engine, 18-seat airliner. Note the total lack of either horizontal or vertical tail surfaces. *(The Boeing Company Archives)*

Each was a pusher. The Northrop XP-56 Black Bullet, built under project MX-14, featured a flying wing configuration of sorts, with a very short bullet-shaped fuselage and no horizontal tail. Like the later B-2, it would feature unusual materials; the XP-56 had an all-welded, all-magnesium structure. Both examples were powered by a single 2,400-hp Pratt & Whitney R-2800 Double Wasp engine spinning two 3-bladed, contra-rotating pusher propellers.

First flown on September 6, 1943, the first XP-56 (which had very little vertical tail area) crashed while taxiing on October 8, 1943. A second example, with a larger vertical tail area,

Northrop also created a number of fighter-type flying wing aircraft, including two prototype XP-56 "Black Bullet" aircraft. This is the first example, shown as it runs up its engine prior to first take-off with famed Northrop test pilot John W. "Polo" Myers at the controls. *(AFFTC/HO)*

The second XP-56 is shown here on Rogers Dry Lake. Both of these model N2B pusher-type experimental pursuit aircraft were powered by a single Pratt & Whitney R-2800 radial engine spinning two 3-bladed contra-rotating propellers. The additional tail area of ship number two is noteworthy. *(AFFTC/HO)*

made its first flight on March 23, 1944, and was much more successful. However, as it turned out, the surviving XP-56 did not have enough maneuverability in simulated dogfights with then state-of-the-art P-38s, P-47s, and P-51s to warrant production.

The MX-324 and MX-334

The MX-324 was a nonpowered semi-flying wing glider that was built to validate the aerodynamics of the near-identical but rocket-powered MX-334 aircraft. In turn, the powered MX-334 was to validate the concept of a rocket-powered interceptor known as the XP-79.

The powered MX-334 Rocket Wing was a semi-flying wing (it had a vertical tail) and was propelled by a single 200-lb thrust Aerojet XCAL-200 rocket motor. It made its first flight on July 5, 1944. Historically, this was the first flight of a rocket-powered airplane in U.S. history. As a test bed for the proposed XP-79, to be powered by a 2,000-lb thrust rocket motor, the MX-334 did an adequate job. Nevertheless, as a wholly underpowered demonstrator, it created serious doubts about the ultimate success of a rocket-powered interceptor.

The XP-79 and XP-79B

Under project MX-365, Northrop was awarded a contract to build three XP-79 prototypes (43-52435/-52437). This trio of semi-flying wing aircraft were to demonstrate the feasibility of producing rocket-powered interceptor aircraft that would use ramming as a combat

The rocket-powered MX-334 "Rocket Wing" as it looked in July 1945. This unique aircraft was essentially the prototype of a proposed rocket-powered interceptor known as the P-79. It made its first flight on July 5, 1945, and thus became the United States' first rocket-powered airplane. *(AFFTC/HO)*

technique. While the three aircraft were under various stages of construction, problems arose with the development of the intended Aerojet XCAL-2000 rocket motor propulsion system. Their development was terminated.

Being the least advanced in construction at the time, the third XP-79 airframe (42-52437) was converted to turbojet power. It was redesignated XP-79B and was completed with two 1,150-lb thrust Westinghouse J30 axial-flow turbojet engines. The XP-79B was intended to lead to the production of P-79B jet-powered interceptors.

This series of semi-flying wing aircraft—MX-324, MX-334, XP-79 and XP-79B—did not have seats for their pilots. The pilot lay prone to enable the pilot to withstand as many as 12 Gs (a 200-lb pilot would weigh 2,400 lb) while maneuvering in combat. Both the non-powered MX-324 glider and the powered MX-334 were flown in this configuration, as was the XP-79B "Flying Ram."

On September 12, 1945, Northrop test pilot Harry Crosby made the first flight of the XP-79B. It flew well for about 15 min. Then, for what remains to be an unexplained reason, the aircraft went into a slow roll and, after a steep vertical spin, flew into the ground. Crosby bailed out but was killed when he was hit by the spinning aircraft.

Although Northrop Aircraft had suffered a number of both explained and unexplained crashes and test-pilot deaths during its early flying wing trials, the Army was still most interested in its XB-35 and YB-35 programs. Therefore, work continued.

The XB-35 and YB-35

Based on the success of the N-9M, two experimental XB-35s and 13 service test YB-35s were ordered under projects MX-140 and MP-13 (*MP* meaning "materiel, prototype"). These were intended as back-up bombardment aircraft in case the preferred Consolidated Vultee Aircraft (Convair) XB-36 failed to perform as advertised. Northrop naturally hoped the B-35 would go into production rather than the B-36. A service test order for 13 YB-35 aircraft followed a contract for two experimental XB-35s.

The XB-35 made its first flight on June 25, 1946, beginning an ill-fated test program that saw many delays. Powered by four 3,000-hp Pratt & Whitney R-4360 engines, fitted with two 4-bladed contra-rotating propellers each, the XB-35 had a projected top speed of 395 mph at 40,000 ft.

Unfortunately, there were problems with the R-4360's propeller gearboxes and engine cooling systems, and it was decided to convert some of the aircraft already under construction to turbojet power. Two YB-35s were taken off Northrop's production line to be finished as the turbojet-powered YB-49s, powered by eight turbojet engines. The USAF officially canceled the B-35 program in November 1949.

The YB-49 and YRB-49A

After demonstrating limited success, the two XB-35s and one of the 13 YB-35 aircraft were scrapped after their respective flight-test programs had ended. Three of the unfinished YB-35s underwent numerous modifications to become the two 8-jet YB-49s and the single six-jet YRB-49A.

On October 21, 1947, the first of two service test Northrop YB-49 bomber aircraft took to the skies over southern California to perform its maiden flight. It, however, had four vertical stabilizers and four ventral

After Northrop received a contract to build a number of experimental XB-35s and service test YB-35s, it proceeded to deliver them. Shown here in this somewhat rare scene are 11 of the 15 XB/YB-35s in various stages of construction. The two at the top are being converted to the jet-powered YB-49s. *(Northrop Grumman)*

An XB-35 on the ramp at Muroc in the late 1940s. It was powered by four Pratt & Whitney R-4360 engines—each one turning two 4-bladed contrarotating propellers. Its successor, the eight-jet YB-49, banks right above it. *(AFFTC/HO)*

fins for increased stability, a departure from the pure lines of the XBs and YB-35s. The YB-49s were powered by eight 3,750-lb thrust General Electric J35 turbojet engines and reached speeds of 500 mph.

Unfortunately for Northrop's YB-49, the first of two Boeing XB-47 Stratojet experimental bombers made its first flight on December 17, 1947. Although the number one YB-49 had

An XB-35 in flight near Edwards (then Muroc) illustrates the fact that it had no horizontal or vertical tails. It was, according to Sgt. Robert Morris, one of its ground crew, "a Maytag washing machine in motion" and "the loudest aircraft I've ever heard." *(AFFTC/HO)*

The immediate predecessor of today's B-2 stealth bomber, albeit some 40 years earlier, was the Northrop YB-49 Flying Wing bomber. Powered by eight General Electric J35 turbojet engines, after many test flights, it was declared too unstable to be an adequate bombardment platform. Its production was therefore terminated. Two examples were built from modified YB-35 aircraft, and the first one made its first flight on October 21, 1947—some 42 years before the B-2A made its flight. *(AFFTC/HO)*

Jack Northrop's final attempt at obtaining a USAF production contract for one of his many flying wing aircraft designs came in the form of the one-of-a-kind YRB-49A. It was created from an unfinished YB-35 and featured four J35s within its wing and another two J35s in pods beneath its wing. As proposed, this was to be a photographic reconnaissance bomber. With a Lockheed TF-80C (later T-33A) flying chase, it is shown during its first flight on May 4, 1950. *(AFFTC/HO)*

been flying for eight months already, the swept wing six-jet Stratojet dominated its competition, which included the four-jet Convair XB-46 and the six-jet Martin XB-48. Testing of the two YB-49s proceeded, with the second example making its first flight on January 13, 1948. On June 5, 1948, the second YB-49 crashed, killing its entire crew. On March 15, 1950, the first example was lost in a high-speed taxiing mishap.

From the ashes of B-35-cum-B-49 came yet one more attempt to put a flying wing aircraft into USAF service—the Northrop YRB-49A, proposed as a six-jet reconnaissance bomber (RB) aircraft. Created from yet another YB-35 airframe, the one-of-a-kind YRB-49A made its first flight on May 4, 1950. However, it too failed to meet USAF requirements and was ultimately scrapped.

With the cancellation of the YRB-49A, Jack Northrop's flying wing aircraft had reached the end of the line. It would not be until the advent of low-observable (stealth) technology for military aircraft that the flying wing concept would reappear.

Another Flying Wing: The A-12 Avenger II

The A-12 Avenger II was to be a carrier-based, air-to-air or air-to-ground, all-weather, day-or-night attack aircraft. It was to replace the U.S. Navy's fleet of Grumman (now Northrop Grumman) A-6E Intruder attack aircraft beginning in the mid-1990s.

As an all-flying wing spanning 70 ft, 3 in, the proposed McDonnell Douglas/General Dynamics (now Boeing/Lockheed Martin) A-12 Avenger II was to accommodate a full range of air-to-ground ordnance. This ordnance included "smart" weapons such as the GBU-10, -12, -15, and -24 laser-guided bombs. *(Lockheed Martin)*

As an advanced technology aircraft (ATA), it was to incorporate even more advanced stealth characteristics than the Lockheed Martin F-117A Nighthawk stealth fighter and was to have an all-flying wing configuration. As a ground-attack weapon system, it was to carry an assortment of the latest air-to-ground ordnance including satellite-guided JDAMs (Joint Direct Attack Munitions). As a medium fighter, it was to be armed with a pair of AIM-120 "Slammer" air-to-air missiles for area- and point-defense of the fleet. For the destruction of ground-based radar installations, it was to carry two AGM-88 high-speed antiradiation missiles (HARM); no cannon or gun was to be carried.

The A-12 was being developed by McDonnell Douglas in St. Louis, Missouri, (now Boeing) and General Dynamics in Fort Worth, Texas, (now Lockheed Martin Tactical Aircraft Systems). However, cost overruns and schedule delays forced Defense Secretary Richard Cheney to cancel the program on January 7, 1991. (At the time, it was the largest contract termination in Defense Department history.)

Over the life of the Avenger II program, the USN had planned to buy 620 of the A-12 aircraft. Eight aircraft

(a) Front view of mockup

(b) Top view of mockup

Only a full-scale engineering mock-up of the Avenger II was built. On air-to-air missions, U.S. Navy A-12s were to carry two AIM-120C "Slammer" AMRAAM (advanced medium-range air-to-air missile). To destroy radar installations, Avenger II aircraft would have been armed with two AGM-88 HARM (high-speed antiradiation missile). *(Lockheed Martin)*

were to be built for the full-scale development (FSD) program. The first lot of six aircraft, funded during fiscal year 1990 (FY90), were to be used to support the operational test and evaluation and fleet introduction of the A-12.

This proposed all-flying wing would have been operated by two crew members and would have been powered by two nonafterburning 13,000-lb thrust General Electric F412-GE-400 turbofan engines. Top speed at sea level was to be 580 mph. In full-scale engineering mock-up form, the Avenger II has a wingspan of 70 ft, 3 in, with a wing area of 1,308 sq ft. It was 37 ft, 3 in long and stood 11 ft, 3 in high. With its wing tips folded upward for carrier stowage, it spanned 36 ft, 3 in. Its gross takeoff weight was to be about 80,000 lb.

The Flying Wing Returns

In the early 1980s the Northrop Corporation once again became a contender for a new breed of bomber—a stealth bomber with a flying wing configuration. The competition was for an Advanced Technology Bomber (ATB) which, after a hard fight, was won by Northrop.

Northrop's initial ATB configuration showed either no vertical tails or two vertical tails mounted at various locations atop its wing planform (inboard or outboard; canted inward) with a W-shaped wing trailing edge layout. A redesign was undertaken and featured a "double W"-shaped trailing edge with no vertical tails. As a pure all-flying wing aircraft, it now met the USAF's goal of creating a stealth bomber capable of either low- or high-altitude penetration missions. This unique aircraft was subsequently designated B-2A and named Spirit.

The B-2 is the world's first and only low-observable (stealth) heavy-bombardment aircraft. This advanced technology bomber was originally conceived as a highly survivable strategic bombardment platform to initially supplement, and ultimately replace, the Boeing North American B-1B Lancer in its penetration role.

Current U.S. Air Force (USAF) operational planning focuses on the B-2's conventional capabilities, employing it as a lead weapon system to be used to bring about the early engagement and destruction of an enemy's war-making assets and potential. Yet, if needed, the B-2 can destroy any enemy on the planet with a powerful nuclear punch.

The pure all-flying wing configuration of the B-2 has a smoothly blended fuselage that accommodates a two-person aircraft operations crew, adequate space for a third person, and a pair of large-volume side-by-side weapons bays in the lower centerbody. Each one of these large-volume weapons bays contains either a rotary launcher or a bomb rack assembly (BRA) able to carry a payload of more than 20,000 lb. Under the Single Integrated Operational Plan (SIOP), about 12,500 lb of nuclear weapons would be a normal payload for each bay.

Mounted in pairs deeply buried within the wing structure are four nonafterburning 17,300-lb thrust turbofan engines, with scalloped overwing air inlets and shielded overwing engine exhaust nozzles. The aircraft features a quadruple-redundant digital fly-by-wire (FBW) flight-control system, actuating a series of movable surfaces at the B-2's trailing edges that include aileron, air brake, elevator, flap, gust alleviation, rudder, and spoiler functions.

At this writing, 20 of 21 B-2s have been delivered to the 509th Bomb Wing at Whiteman Air Force Base (AFB), Missouri; the 509th being comprised of two combat squadrons and one training squadron. Within their first four years of service, operational B-2s have achieved a mission-capable rate of 90 percent. Under current USAF plans, the twenty-first and last B-2 is scheduled for its delivery to Whiteman Air Force Base, Missouri, sometime in the year 2000.

The B-2's low-observable characteristics mean that it does not need an armada of support aircraft to accomplish its mission, and its large payload allows it to do the work of many smaller attack-type aircraft. The USAF has published a representative mission scenario showing that two B-2s armed with 16 precision weapons can do the job of a package of 75 conventional aircraft (comprised of bombers, radar jammers, radar busters, airborne tankers, and escort fighters). Therefore, four crewpersons are put at risk in this mission, compared to 132 crewpersons in the conventional aircraft package.

After takeoff, a B-2 can fly more than 6,000 nmi on its internal fuel supply alone. With just one aerial refueling en route, it can fly more than 10,000 nmi. This gives it the ability to fly from secure bases in the United States to any point on the globe within a matter of hours.

The B-2 Spirit can carry more than 20 tons (40,000 lb) of conventional or nuclear ordnance and deliver it accurately day or night in any weather condition. A single B-2 can deliver sixteen 2,000-lb near-precision, and soon full-precision, munitions. More important, a lone B-2 stealth bomber can do the work of eight Lockheed Martin F-117A Nighthawk stealth fighters.

The B-2's nuclear, conventional, and precision weapons tests have all gone extremely well. Therefore, the USAF was able to announce an early, but limited, initial operational capability (IOC) for the B-2 weapon system. Full IOC for the first combat squadron of B-2s (393rd BS) was declared on April 1, 1997. To this end, for the first time in military aviation history, the USAF has a war-fighting capability that combines large-payload, long-range, stealth, and both near- and full-precision weapons deliveries all in one aircraft. Whether flying at 200 or 50,000 ft above ground level, whether carrying a bellyful of conventional or nuclear weapons, the Northrop Grumman B-2A Spirit truly is the most capable war machine on the planet.

Classified as a heavy, multimission bomber, the Northrop Grumman B-2A Spirit is optimized to enhance the strategic capabilities of the USAF and its Air Combat Command (ACC). It is being both missionized and optimized to complement the USAF's existing fleets of Boeing B-52H Stratofortresses and Boeing North American B-1B Lancers.

In one deadly scenario, a single B-2A, armed with sixteen 2,000-lb class GBU-31 Joint Direct Attack Munition (JDAM) conventional high-explosive warhead weapons, can completely destroy 16 hardened targets such as command, control, and communications centers, surface-to-air missile sites, radar installations, or weapons manufacturing facilities. In another scenario, too terrible to imagine, a lone B-2 armed with sixteen 1-2 MT nuclear B83 bombs could destroy that many cities within any aggressor's nation.

Developmental Highlights

"It is difficult to stipulate in advance the precise number of [bomber] aircraft in the fleet which must be stealthy, but it is surely more than 21 B-2s . . ."

—GENERAL RUSSELL E. DOUGHERTY, USAF, RETIRED

The development of the Northrop Grumman B-2A Spirit can be traced back to June 30, 1977, when President Jimmy Carter canceled the B-1A Advanced Manned Strategic Aircraft production program. President Carter ordered that no production B-1As would be built, but that the three prototype B-1As that had been built would continue their respective flight-test and weapon systems evaluation programs—although at a reduced level of activity. Carter believed that the upcoming air-launched cruise missile (ALCM) weapons could more effectively deter nuclear aggression and that the redirected B-1A production moneys would be better used on a program to modify existing Boeing B-52G/H Stratofortress bomber aircraft to carry and deliver the ALCMs. (A fourth B-1A was built and flown in 1979.)

To maintain the most flexible leg of the United States' Strategic Triad policy, these ALCM-armed B-52G/Hs were to work in concert with some 70 General Dynamics FB-111As—the United States's only other operational strategic bombardment aircraft at the time—as well as the submarine- and silo-launched intermediate and intercontinental ranging ballistic missiles.

The Carter administration's decision to terminate Rockwell International's B-1A production program (some 240 examples were to be built) drew vast amounts of heat from many sources. Carter was able to hold firm on his decision because, unknown to most politicians and the general public, he had an ace up his sleeve that had been passed on to him in late 1975 by the Ford administration. Unfortunately, for Carter, it was an ace he could not play at the time, for it was as secret as the Manhattan Project of World War II had been. The secret was stealth technology.

The first of four North American Rockwell (now Boeing North American) B-1A prototypes as it appeared the night before its October 26, 1974, rollout ceremony at Palmdale, California. The USAF, its Strategic Air Command in particular, had wanted to procure some 240 production B-1As. However, in June 1977, President Carter canceled B-1 production, and only the four B-1A prototypes were ever built. *(Boeing North American)*

Some seven years after the premier B-1A prototype appeared, President Reagan announced that a highly modified version of the B-1A—the B-1B—would be built. Thus, by mid-1988, USAF/SAC had taken delivery of 100 production B-1B Lancers. As a matter of interest, after some 13 years of operational service, the B-1B was first used in a combat on December 18, 1998, during the four-day air campaign against Iraq in Operation Desert Fox. *(Boeing North American)*

Basic Formula for Stealth

There is a basic formula in the creation of a successful stealth aircraft. By using computerized three-dimensional graphics design, a successful stealth aircraft design can be created in which its shape alone will account for 85 percent of its success in avoiding radar detection. It must also possess other low-observable characteristics to avoid detection by reducing infrared (heat), acoustic (sound), contrail (engine exhaust trail), and electromagnetic (avionics) signatures.

To ward off the advances being made by ever-improving radar systems, a dedicated stealth aircraft must have a very, very low radar cross section (RCS). Measured in square meters (1 sq m equals 1.196 sq yd), the RCS of a stealth aircraft must approach zero. In other words, the aircraft in question must not appear larger than a small bird on a radar screen.

The venerable but still operational B-52H has an RCS equal to about 60 sq m, while the B-1B measures 0.6 of 1 sq m—an impressive reduction. Yet the RCS of an F-117 is reportedly as low as 0.1 of 1 sq m. The B-2, much larger than the F-117, has a reported RCS of less than .06 of 1 sq m.

After shaping, the second most important aspect in controlling RCS is the use of radar-absorbing materials (RAM), radar-absorbing structures (RAS), and the proper placement of the aircraft's engine air inlets and ducting, engines, and engine exhaust nozzles. The latter is extremely critical to the overall success of a stealth aircraft.

Engine placement deep within a stealth aircraft's body is imperative. The B-2's cleverly designed and configured engine air inlets, followed by snakelike air ducts, effectively hide the large engine faces from radar. While unique engine exhaust nozzles not only hide the large engine rear ends from radar, they help to reduce both engine noise and heat levels. In addition, the use of nonaugmented (afterburning) engines reduces excessive thermal (heat) signatures.

The first real attempt of reducing an aircraft's RCS came in the form of the Lockheed A-12, the progenitor of the famed Lockheed SR-71 "Blackbird," which is considered to be the first generation of stealth aircraft. These aircraft were created to supplant and possibly replace the Lockheed U-2, which on July 4, 1956, began overflying the Soviet Union on secret Central Intelligence Agency (CIA) missions. The USSR fired surface-to-air missiles (SAMs) at them, but the SAMs of the day did not have enough range to reach the U-2s at their 70,000-ft or more operating altitudes.

Things rapidly changed, however. Between mid-1956 and early 1960, Russia developed improved radars and longer-ranging SAMs, and on May 1, 1960, the Lockheed U-2C being flown by Francis Gary "Frank" Powers was not only tracked but shot down. Powers survived the ordeal, but this event caused a major political uproar and could have escalated into something far worse. The event also gave further urgency to the Lockheed A-12 Oxcart program just starting development.

Instead of flying high and slow like the U-2, the A-12 was to fly even higher (up to 80,000 ft) and much, much faster—at three times the speed of sound. With its greatly reduced RCS and triplesonic speed at more than 15 mi altitude, the A-12 was to be more survivable.

Unlike the slow U-2, by the time that an A-12 was discovered and a missile fired, it would be out of range.

A small number of A-12s were used by the CIA, as covert overflights became the way of life. Under the Senior Crown program, an improved version of the Lockheed A-12 materialized in the form of the Lockheed SR-71A. Unofficially named "Blackbird" because of its all-black paint scheme, the SR-71 had similar performance as the A-12 but an even lower RCS. The SR-71's RCS has been rumored to be about that of an upright 6-ft-tall man, quite small for an aircraft that measures more than 107 ft long, spans more than 55 ft, stands some 18 ft high, and weighs more than 170,000 lb.

The many successes of the now-retired SR-71A Blackbird are well known, and though some were lost, not one was ever shot down. Moreover, the success of the SR-71 reconnaissance aircraft led to the creation of the "second generation" of operational stealth airplanes—the Lockheed F-117 Nighthawk, the world's first and still only dedicated low-observable attack bombardment aircraft. Classified as a stealth fighter, the F-117's creation depended on the success of Lockheed's Have Blue program.

Considered the first generation of operational stealth aircraft, the Lockheed Martin SR-71A "Blackbird" is probably the most exotic airplane that was ever built and flown. With its inward-canted vertical tails made of composite materials, engine nacelle and fuselage chines, and a host of other 'trick' features, the SR-71A survived many years of operational service without ever being shot down. It also was very fast. For example: One of its VIP guest pilots, none other than Chuck Yeager, flew one to a speed of Mn 3.23 at 78,000 ft. *(Lockheed Martin Skunk Works)*

Have Blue, Tacit Blue, and Senior Trend

Serious investigations into stealth-capable aircraft began in the early 1970s with a combined USAF and Defense Advanced Research Projects Agency (DARPA) program called Have Blue. Ultimately, Lockheed and Northrop became the two finalists in that unique program in which they were to each build two flyable test bed aircraft. The aim was to provide an unprecedented survivability against the best radar systems known to humankind. At the end of the competition, Lockheed was given the green light.

The two Lockheed Have Blue aircraft ultimately proved that stealth worked—and that stealth aircraft, with their unusual configuration, could fly. This resulted in the creation of the Lockheed F-117A Nighthawk stealth fighter under the Senior Trend program.

Though Northrop had lost the stealth fighter contract, it was able to continue its stealthy aircraft design work through its Tacit Blue program. The Tacit Blue aircraft was an unconventional design, but it pioneered a number of significant breakthroughs in shaping and structural designs that are used in the B-2 Spirit of today (see Chap. 3). Northrop's whale-like Tacit Blue aircraft began life in December 1976 as a DARPA program first called Assault Breaker and then Battlefield Surveillance Aircraft, Experimental (BSAX). By mid-1977, after failing a number of radar pole measurements, Northrop's radar test model of the BSAX was in trouble. By late 1977, after using some 100 lb of clay to reshape the aircraft's configuration, Northrop electromagneticist Fred Oshira discovered the correct shape for Tacit Blue.

Now featuring walled sides, sloping downward to putty-knifelike edges, the Tacit Blue radar pole model easily passed its RCS tests. Thus, Northrop was given the green light to build two examples of Tacit Blue—one for flight testing and one to serve as a spare airframe.

The only flyable Tacit Blue (Whale) aircraft was originally created to demonstrate that a manned low-observable (stealth) surveillance aircraft with a low probability of intercept (LPI) radar system and other sensors could operate close to the forward line of battle with a high degree of survivability. It proved that such an aircraft could continuously monitor the ground situation behind the battle lines and provide targeting information in real time to battlefield commanders.

Tacit Blue made its first flight in February 1982 and went on to log 134 more flights over a three-year period. In the end the Tacit Blue program provided valuable engineering data that aided in the design of the B-2 Spirit. This program remained classified until April 30, 1996, and the aircraft is now on permanent display at the USAF Museum in Dayton, Ohio.

Have Blue/Tacit Blue

Earlier in 1974 under Project Harvey, a DARPA-funded program was initiated to investigate the possibility of creating an aircraft—a manned fighter-bomber, with a very low or nonexistent RCS. It was to be a plane that could penetrate the airspace of an enemy without detection, then take out ground-to-air missile and radar sites as a prelude to gaining and maintaining air superiority. Initially, however, to prove or disprove the project, DARPA did not require that the aircraft be constructed with either avionics or weapons systems.

Begun as a relatively high-priority but low-funded program, without any assurance of an aircraft production order, Project Harvey moved into the beginning of 1975. In January of that year, DARPA awarded two study contracts to Northrop and McDonnell Douglas. Lockheed got wind of the program and prepared an unsolicited proposal with its own funds.

McDonnell Douglas's low RCS effort fell short, and in September 1975, Lockheed and Northrop were issued contracts to design an Experimental Survivable Test Bed (XST). DARPA instructed both airframe contractors that the winner of the impending radar pole "fly-off" would build two XST aircraft—one for flight test and the other for RCS tests. As required, each firm subsequently built a full-scale XST model, and these were thoroughly evaluated at the USAF's radar cross-section range somewhere within the boundaries of Holloman AFB, New Mexico. These RCS models, though built to full scale, were actually about two-thirds the size of what an actual production aircraft would be.

Following many RCS evaluations of both XST entries, Lockheed emerged victorious. In March 1976, now with the USAF on board, Lockheed received a contract to build two XST demonstrator aircraft under what was now called Have Blue. Because of the unprecedented shaping of Lockheed's entry, with its flat plates and jutted angles, one example was to be used for flight testing alone. Simply put, Lockheed's XST did not look like it would fly. If it proved it could fly, however, the other Have Blue XST aircraft would be used for dedicated low-RCS evaluations.

The two Lockheed Have Blue aircraft measured more than 47 ft long, 7 ft high, and spanned more than 22 ft, with a wing area of 386 sq ft. Their semi-delta wings swept aft at an astounding 72.5 degrees. In addition, they featured two inward-canted vertical stabilizers; the all-movable top half of each tail served as rudders. Fully fueled, each example weighed about 12,500 lb, and each airplane was powered by two nonafterburning General Electric J85-GE-4A turbojet engines.

With Lockheed test pilot William M. "Bill" Park at the controls, the first prototype XST (Lockheed Serial Number 1001) made its first flight on December 1, 1977, somewhere within the Nellis AFB, Nevada, test range complex. It went on to fly another 35 missions before it crashed on May 4, 1978, because of an in-flight landing gear malfunction. With its fully computerized fly-by-wire (FBW) flight control system, the number one XST successfully served as an aerodynamic test air vehicle and proved that an extremely unorthodox aircraft could actually fly.

Just after its completion (sans paint), looking like no aircraft seen heretofore, the first of two Have Blue XST aircraft awaits its initial flight. First flown on December 1, 1977, by Lockheed test pilot Bill Park, this unique aircraft—with its digital fly-by-wire flight control system, proved beyond a doubt that such an unorthodox airplane could actually fly. *(Lockheed Martin Skunk Works)*

The second prototype XST, the radar cross-section test air vehicle (Lockheed S/N 1002), made its first flight on July 20, 1978, with USAF Col. Norman K. "Ken" Dyson in its seat. It made another 51 flights, but it too was lost in a crash on July 24, 1979, due to an engine fire.

The Lockheed XST aircraft had accomplished their respective goals. While the number one aircraft proved that a faceted aircraft could indeed fly well, the number two bird proved that stealth, or low-observable, technology really worked against the best radar systems. After their respective crashes, both of these trend-setting stealth aircraft were quietly buried somewhere under the desert terrain of Nellis's test ranges.

Enter Senior Trend—The F-117A Stealth Fighter

With a total of 86 successful test hops between them— two additional flights ending in crashes—the two Lockheed XST aircraft opened the secret gateway that had been hiding the unknown mystery of how to effectively defeat modern radar systems. The USAF proceeded with the next phase of its stealth aircraft program. By October 1979, under the Senior Trend program, Lockheed had, in deepest secrecy, begun to build and fly five FSD stealth fighter aircraft known as Scorpion 1 through Scorpion 5. At about the same time, on October 15, 1979, the 4450th Tactical Group (TG) was formed at Nellis AFB. As a ploy to hide its true purpose in life, the 4450th TG was equipped with a number of Ling-Temco-Vought (LTV) A-7D Corsair II attack aircraft that, when equipped with Scorpion 1 to 5-type systems, doubled as stealth fighter training aircraft.

As the Senior Trend program moved ahead, the USAF pondered upon a designation for the aircraft that would not give the secret aircraft program away. Since

This highly detailed top view of Scorpion 1, the first of five Senior Trend full-scale development aircraft, dramatically illustrates the aircraft's vast array of angular surfaces. Unlike production F-117s, Scorpion 1 featured the use of an instrumented nose boom, as well as the standard four flight data probes. The aircraft's extreme wing sweep angle is noteworthy. *(Lockheed Martin Skunk Works)*

The success of the two Have Blue XST aircraft and the five FSD Scorpion aircraft led to the production of 59 operational F-117A Nighthawk stealth fighters. There were those who seriously doubted the highly touted survivability of the F-117 aircraft, but its success in Operation Desert Storm eliminated all of those doubts. The F-117 is considered the second-generation operational stealth aircraft. *(Lockheed Martin Skunk Works)*

it was to be a light-attack bombardment aircraft rather than a fighter, the designation A-11 was suggested. The designation would follow Fairchild Republic (formerly Republic) A-10 Thunderbolt II. This suggested designation was quickly dropped because it conflicted with the Lockheed A-11 (an aircraft announced to exist by President Johnson back in 1964; it was actually the Lockheed YF-12A Improved Manned Interceptor [IMI] prototype aircraft).

The next considerations centered around either F-19 or F/A-19 to follow the designation already applied to the McDonnell/Northrop F/A-18 Hornet. Then Northrop created the F-5G Tigershark, which the USAF redesignated as the F-20A. As a result, the USAF abandoned the F-19 designation for its upcoming stealth aircraft. The USAF could honestly answer that it had no stealth fighter designated F-19. Finally, the USAF opted for the designation F-117A.

The reason it selected the designation F-117A was two-fold: First, since late 1962 in an effort to eliminate high-digit designation numbers and interservice confusion, fighter aircraft designations had been recycled to start anew at number one, or F-1. Second, since the last designation had ended at F-111 before the change, the USAF was confident that no one would ever suspect a new fighter with such a high-digit designation. The USAF's ploy worked very well. It was not until early 1991, some two and a half years after the existence of this unique aircraft was made public, that the stealth fighter was able to prove its advanced technology in combat.

Over the course of the Persian Gulf War, or Operation Desert Storm, a total of 42 F-117s operating from King Khalid Air Base near Khamis Mushait, in the extreme southwestern corner of Saudi Arabia, were extraordinarily effective. The 42 F-117s of the 37th Tactical Fighter Wing (now 49th Fighter Wing) used in Desert Storm represented only 2 percent of total Allied tactical air assets. They flew 1,271 combat sorties, less than 1 percent of the sorties flown by Coalition aircraft. Yet, in a devastating demonstration of air power, the F-117s delivered more than 2,000 tons of precision-guided munitions with such unprecedented accuracy that they accounted for 40 percent of all strategic targets attacked, achieving better than a 75 percent direct-hit rate. Despite fierce Iraqi defenses, not a single F-117 ever experienced damage from enemy fire. This success was attributable to its low-observability (stealth) technology.

Stealthy Fighters to Stealthy Bombers

The extraordinary capabilities of the ALCM that President Carter had backed was never in doubt, and there were never any ALCM-versus-manned bomber debates. Instead, many questioned the venerable B-52's ability to soldier on indefinitely with the ALCMs, since the newest B-52, an H model, had been procured in fiscal year 1961. Skeptics wondered if the fleet of Stratofortresses would be flying long enough to undergo their modification program to incorporate ALCMs into their weapon system. The FB-111A would not be able to carry ALCMs—period.

While the Carter-ordered B-52G/H ALCM modification program moved ahead, the U.S. Air Force launched a number of manned bomber design studies under its Sabre Penetrator

Likened to a flying barn as far as its RCS is concerned, the Boeing B-52H Stratofortress is the last version of the BUFF (Big, Ugly, Fat Fellow) in operational service. The B-52 has soldiered on since its operational debut in 1955. Its survivability, however, is due to its use of electronic counter-measures and not stealth. *(Boeing)*

program in an effort to find an adequate B-52 replacement. These studies created a multitude of new Air Force acronyms: MRB for Multi-Role Bomber; SWL for Strategic Weapons Launcher; NTP for Near-Term Penetrator; LRCA for Long-Range Combat Aircraft; and CMCA for Cruise Missile Carrier Aircraft. These proposed bomber studies ran the gamut during the 1978 to 1979 time period and generated aircraft configurations ranging from high-and-fast to low-and-slow penetrating types. Some of these featured semi- and all-flying wing configurations, while some had no wings at all.

Existing commercial jetliner aircraft were even studied as CMCA types. These included the wide-bodied Boeing 747, Lockheed L-1011, and McDonnell Douglas DC-10. However, due to their immense radar cross sections, the notion of these blimplike aircraft hovering around enemy airspace with ALCMs onboard was ludicrous. Operational B-52s, and the canceled B-1A itself, would obviously be more appropriate air vehicles to carry and deliver ALCMs. The proposed CMCA was quickly passed over.

For near-term application, it boiled down to a dual between two proposed aircraft: (1) A significantly modified B-1A known as the Long-Range Combat Aircraft (LRCA), and (2) A stretched F-111 known as the FB-111H. While General Dynamics and Rockwell International fought hard to win production contracts for their respective FB-111H and B-1B (as the LRCA was designated) aircraft, several occurrences wounded Jimmy Carter's bid for reelection. The first of these came on November 4, 1979, when Iranian militants seized the American Embassy in Teheran, Iran, and kept its numerous occupants hostage. The second happened on April 25, 1980, when a number of American servicemen were either killed or wounded during a failed hostage rescue attempt. The third event came about in mid-1980.

At the time, to most everyone's disbelief, the previously mentioned ace President Carter had been holding was shown to the entire world. America's top secret low-observable, or stealth, bomber program was revealed, leading to speculation about a stealth fighter program. Many believed this so-called leak from the White House was criminal, and an explanation was in high demand. National security had been breached and a House Armed Services Committee investigation of "who leaked what to whom about America's so-called stealth (invisible) bomber program" ensued. Additionally, with this technologically advanced aerial weapon system ace called stealth now out of the hole, it was time for agonizing reappraisal.

Considered the third generation of operational stealth aircraft, the B-2 Spirit uses every aspect of stealth design known to humanity. A single B-2 can do the work of eight F-117 Nighthawks. The seventh operational B-2A, the Spirit of NEBRASKA (89-0128) is shown. *(Northrop Grumman)*

The fourth-generation stealth aircraft, not yet operational, is the Lockheed Martin/Boeing F-22A Raptor shown here with Lockheed Martin F-22 Chief Test Pilot Paul Metz. This first of nine engineering, manufacturing, and development (EMD) Raptors is currently undergoing extensive flight-test activities at Edwards AFB. Although it is roughly the same size as an F-117A, the F-22A is reportedly more stealthy. *(Lockheed Martin Aeronautical Systems)*

President Carter lost his bid for a second term, and Ronald Reagan was elected as the United States' next president. Moreover, as a dedicated believer in a strong United States, Reagan decided to build 100 Rockwell B-1Bs. However, the stealth secret was out in the open, and to deal with it in part—while still keeping the stealth fighter program secret—the Reagan administration announced the Advanced Technology Bomber (ATB) program.

Origins of the Advanced Technology Bomber

Earlier, because both the flight test and low RCS evaluations of the Lockheed XST aircraft had been successful and the production of F-117 stealth fighters was underway, the Carter administration had secretly originated a stealth bomber program in 1979. Following the evaluations of request for proposals (RFP) ATB offerings from some of America's leading airframe contractors, the ATB competition narrowed to two teams. These teams, headed by Lockheed and Northrop, were issued study contracts to investigate development and production of such a weapon system.

CHAPTER
3

Senior Ice versus Senior Peg

"The Lockheed/Rockwell ATB proposal was essentially a scaled up Black Jet [F-117A stealth fighter] roughly the size of a B-58 with four engines and two crew."
—AN ANONYMOUS USAF STAFF OFFICER, LATE 1992

After its evaluations of each airframe contractor's proposal, the Department of Defense (DoD) finalized its decision upon who would actually compete in the Advanced Technology Bomber (ATB) competition. It would be Lockheed and Northrop, due to their extensive experiences on the development of stealthy aircraft—the Lockheed Have Blue and Northrop Tacit Blue. Subsequently, the DoD code-named the two ATB programs.

Code-named Senior Ice, the proposed Northrop-led team's ATB was in direct competition with the Lockheed-led team's Senior Peg ATB proposal. As far as the ATB airframe competition was concerned, Northrop teamed up with Boeing, and Lockheed teamed up with Rockwell. General Electric and Pratt & Whitney competed to see which one of them would provide the ATB's propulsion system.

The Lockheed/Rockwell ATB entry was based upon Lockheed's experience with its still highly classified Have Blue XST and F-117A aircraft. It was similarly configured as the F-117A, but with four engines instead of two. It looked very much like an F-117A, but was some 95 ft long with a wingspan of about 60 ft and a gross takeoff weight of around 200,000 lb.

On the other hand, the Northrop/Boeing ATB design was a wholly different design featuring a W-shaped semi-flying wing configuration with two vertical tails. It also featured the use of four engines and two crew, but it was to be about 70 ft long, with a wingspan of around 170 ft and a gross takeoff weight of about 350,000 lb.

Aurora

The existence of an aircraft intended to replace the SR-71 has been widely reported, including in a book entitled *Aurora: The Pentagon's Secret Hypersonic Spyplane.* The Aurora was supposed to be a top secret, very high altitude (100,000-plus ft), and extremely fast (Mn 6+) photographic reconnaissance and mapping aircraft that would replace the now Lockheed SR-71A "Blackbird." This was not so, according to the late Benjamin R. "Ben" Rich (second president of the famed Lockheed Martin Skunk Works). In his 1994 autobiography with Leo Janos entitled *Skunk Works,* he stated that "it [Aurora] was the B-2 competition funding code" for the Northrop- and Lockheed-led team's ATB proposals.

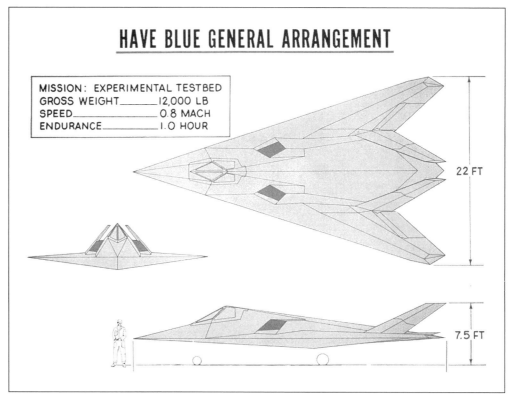

HAVE BLUE GENERAL ARRANGEMENT

MISSION: EXPERIMENTAL TESTBED
GROSS WEIGHT_____12,000 LB
SPEED_____0.8 MACH
ENDURANCE_____1.0 HOUR

22 FT

7.5 FT

Roughly two-thirds the size of the F-117 stealth fighter, Lockheed's Have Blue was 38 ft long, compared to the F-117's length of 65 ft, 11 in. The two Have Blue aircraft were flown 88 times, and during those flights, not only did they prove that an unorthodox design could fly, they proved that stealth worked. *(USAF)*

This relatively rare close-up view of Have Blue number two—the low-observable evaluation test bed—illustrates the aircraft's almost unreal design. Both aircraft crashed and were buried somewhere within the Nellis AFB, Nevada, test ranges. Since these aircraft are so significant to the success of stealth, at least one of them should be dug up, restored, and put on display. *(Lockheed Martin)*

Its landing gear down and locked, F-117A number 804 is on final approach to Tonopah in September 1991. This was the first, and the best, bottom view of an F-117 ever photographed. *(Tony Landis Photo)*

This rare conceptual illustration of a Rockwell (now Boeing North American) stealth fighter/attack design shows unusual engine air inlets and exhaust nozzle features. *(Boeing North American)*

This 1978-era semi-flying wing ATB offering came from Rockwell. Note the wing leading-edge engine air inlets, ventral engine exhaust fairings, and its four ventral fins. *(Boeing North American)*

In this head-on view, offering shades of the B-2 (cockpit canopy windows), the YF-23A (all-moving combination of rudders and elevators), and not much of anything else, the Tacit Blue (Whale) shows off its two uniquely curved tails. Note the aircraft's knife-edged chines. *(Northrop Grumman)*

Originally developed as a Battlefield Surveillance Aircraft-Experimental (BSAX), the Tacit Blue air vehicle proved that such a design could survive behind enemy lines. Its RCS, somewhere near the signature of a bat, proved that more-rounded shaping (note upper fuselage) could also be used for stealth. Thus, the B-2. *(Northrop Grumman)*

Ultimately, the Northrop-led team won the ATB competition, and the so-called Aurora—other than in book and scale model forms—did not materialize. Although many still believe in it, the heavily rumored Aurora aircraft does not exist.

Designing and Engineering the ATB

Designing and engineering the ATB was not an easy task. After it received the ATB contract in October 1981, Northrop Corporation formed its ATB (later B-2) Division. The $36.6 billion contract (FY82 dollars) covered the production of two static airframes and six flying FSD aircraft. The program, still very top secret, was code-named Senior CJ. The initials *CJ*, instead of some random computer-generated name found with other Senior programs such as Senior Trend, referred to a Pentagon stealth program office secretary named Connie Jo Kelly.

Dr. John F. Cashen would play a very large part in Northrop's ATB success. Born on April 14, 1937, in West Orange, New Jersey, Cashen joined Northrop in 1973 as a senior research engineer at the Northrop Research and Technology Center in Rolling Hills Estates, California. Cashen moved to the Aircraft Division the following year and was appointed manager of observables design in 1975. As his prowess in stealth became more and more obvious, Dr. Cashen was promoted to vice president of advanced design and technology with Northrop's Advanced Systems Division, which was renamed the B-2 Division in 1988. He served in that capacity until his early retirement at the age of 55 in February 1993. Nicknamed "Dr. Stealth," John Cashen, along with three other members of the Northrop team that designed the B-2, was corecipient of the 1989 American Institute of Aeronautics and Astronautics' Aircraft Design Award.

Another key player in the B-2 program is Irving T. "Irv" Waaland. Waaland joined Northrop in 1974 as an advanced design project engineer. In 1979 he formed and led the design team for the ATB-cum-B-2. From 1983 to 1986 he served as vice president-technical and subsequently vice president-engineering and advanced projects. He was named Northrop Aircraft Division's chief designer in 1988. In 1991, Mr. Waaland became vice president and chief designer at Northrop Corporation's Advanced Technology and Design Center in Pico Rivera, California. Born July 2, 1927, in Brooklyn, New York, Irv Waaland is now retired.

Waaland, called "Mr. B-2," received the American Defense Preparedness Association's prestigious Simon Award in 1990 for outstanding work in the design and development of advanced weapons systems and, in particular, the B-2. In addition, Mr. Waaland and three other Northrop designers received the American Institute of Aeronautics and Astronautics (AIAA) Design Award in 1989 for their "innovative technical and managerial leadership" that resulted in the development of the B-2.

Genesis of Stealth Aircraft Technology

Ever since the invention and application of precise radar (radio detection and ranging) systems in the early 1940s, the numerous nations equipped with military aircraft have attempted to hide them from these detection systems. The goal was to create certain types

A few weeks before the premier B-2 was unveiled in November 1988, the USAF released this artist concept of what the aircraft was to look like. As it turned out, the actual B-2 looked very much like this illustration. *(USAF)*

of military aircraft—attack, bomber, unmanned aerial drone, fighter, and reconnaissance—that would be invisible to radar. With the advent of Lockheed's U-2 and follow-on SR-71 photographic reconnaissance aircraft, by the mid-1960s, the word *stealth* was being heard in certain circles.

Neither of the aforementioned aircraft were completely stealthy, but each one certainly has a much lower radar cross section than their reconnaissance predecessors. More important, they built the foundation to support the United States' growing fleets of low-observable, or stealth, aircraft.

In comparison with the F-117 Nighthawk, the B-2 Spirit is a very different aircraft. Although they both feature hidden engine air inlets and exhausts, their wing leading-edge sweepback angles are dissimilar. Whereas the F-117 has tails, the B-2 has none. In addition, the F-117 features a W-shaped wing trailing edge, while the B-2 offers a double W shape. *(Northrop Grumman)*

Two Novel Approaches to Stealth

During a press conference on November 10, 1988, at the Pentagon, Defense Department spokesman Dan Howard verified the *actual* existence of the long-rumored stealth fighter. With very few details, and the release of only one poor-quality photograph, the world became aware of the Lockheed F-117A. Its appearance, however, was surprising. While most interested parties believed in the existence of a stealth fighter, it had been assumed that it would have rounded and smoothed features. Instead, it had jutted and angled lines, called *faceting,* much different than the famous "F-19" model kit that received so much attention in the press. In fact, Northrop, through its research with its own Have Blue XST and Tacit Blue (Whale) aircraft, opted for an aircraft with curvaceous lines, completely different from the F-117's highly unorthodox appearance—and not unlike the F-19 model.

The F-117 stealth fighter, replete with angular flat plate lines and saw-toothed leading edges showed that the Skunk Work's approach to low-observable technology was successful. On the other hand, the B-2 stealth bomber, featuring scalloped, rounded, and compound curved lines, in addition to subtle rolling-wave and saw-toothed leading edges, works just as well against the very same radar evaluations.

Ready or Not:
Here Comes the Advanced
Technology Bomber

**"... Responsiveness—the ability to project power
quickly, accurately, and decisively ... anywhere ...
anytime—is the essence of airpower."**

—SHEILA E. WIDNALL, SECRETARY OF THE AIR FORCE

On Tuesday November 22, 1988, the then Northrop Corporation retracted its assembly building doors and slowly towed the first B-2 (82-1066) out for its official rollout ceremony. At Northrop's Site 4 facility on the grounds of USAF Plant 42 in Palmdale, California, more than 1,000 USAF officers, politicians, aerospace industry executives, factory workers, and media members witnessed the invitation-only event.

On November 22, 1988, some seven years and one month after the Northrop-led team had been notified that it had won the ATB competition, the premier B-2 rolled out of Northrop's Site 4 facility located at USAF Plant 42, in Palmdale, California. *(USAF)*

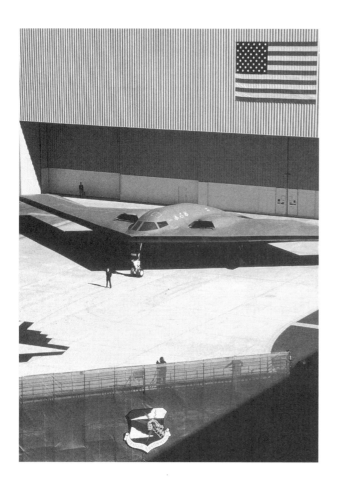

At the time of the aircraft's public debut, the USAF did not want the B-2's peerless saw-toothed trailing edges to be detailed. However, in this particular view, cleared by the USAF itself, the B-2's unique trailing edges are partially visible. *(USAF)*

Rollout

Only after the all-flying wing B-2 had fully emerged from its hangar did those in attendance fully appreciate what they were looking at. Amongst the first things they noticed was the aircraft's lack of any vertical tail surfaces, the wide 172-ft wingspan that features a supercritical airfoil, scalloped engine air inlets, and low stance. Painted in its all black livery, it looked very sinister indeed.

What the audience could not see, however, was its aft end. That view was still secret. A large part of the aircraft's stealth capabilities, as it happens, is its serrated, or saw-toothed, trailing edges. Thus, in its attempt to keep that part of aircraft more secret than the rest, the USAF tried to keep its aft end from view. The USAF's ploy went for nothing, though, because the next issue of *Aviation Week and Space Technology* magazine showed a photograph of the aircraft that had been

As it stands directly behind the Northrop-led team's logo—featuring five B-2s in a star-shaped arrangement—B-2 number one (82-1066) shows off to the world during its first public appearance. Incidentally, the aircraft profiles in the logo fully illustrated the B-2's "secret" trailing edges. *(Northrop Grumman)*

From the intentional placement of the surrounding bleacher sections, it is obvious that USAF officials did not want uninvited eyes to see B-2 number one during its initial debut. Yet hours later a series of rollout photographs became available to the public at large. *(USAF via Chris Wamsley)*

taken from directly overhead during the rollout ceremony, in which a view of its aft end was fully visible.

First Flight

Before any new air vehicle is cleared to fly for its very first time, it must first undergo a series of low-, medium-, and high-speed taxi tests to make sure that brakes, flying control surfaces, nose wheel steering, and other equipment are all working properly (Fig. 4-7). This was true for the B-2. In its first series of taxi tests on July 10, 1989, it reached a maximum ground speed of 103 mph. A number of other taxi runs ensued, and six days later, the premier B-2 was given the green light for flight by USAF B-2 program director Brig. Gen. Richard M. Scofield.

At 6:37 a.m. PDT on July 17, 1989, the world's first stealth bomber rolled down Runway 04 for 4,500 ft before it rotated, lifted off, and flew away from Palmdale on its maiden flight. At the controls sat Chief Test Pilot for Northrop's B-2 Division Bruce J. Hinds and USAF Director of the B-2 Combined Test Force (CTF) Col. Richard S. Couch. Mr. Hinds was in the left seat and served as aircraft commander, while Col. Couch was right-seat test pilot.

Bruce Hinds served in the USAF from 1961 to 1982 and was selected for the rank of colonel when he joined Northrop in 1982 as chief test pilot at the B-2 Division. Hinds has more than 30 years and over 11,000 hours of flight experience. Besides the B-2, he has flown 66 types

With the imposingly large B-2 in their background, airframe contractors and USAF officials spoke to the numerous invited guests in attendance. At the microphone is Northrop President and CEO Thomas V. Jones. Earlier when the time had come to open the doors, T.V. Jones most appropriately said, "Jack Northrop, we salute you." *(USAF via Chris Wamsley)*

(a)

(b)

In the ever-changing world of aerospace, company buyouts and mergers are a way of life. When the first B-2 appeared, its manufacturing team was led by the Northrop Corporation. When the last B-2 appeared, its manufacturing team was led by the Northrop Grumman Corporation, as Northrop had merged with Grumman Aerospace in the interim. Shown here side by side are the (a) pre- and (b) post-merger B-2 Team logos. *(Northrop/Northrop Grumman)*

Selected to make the first B-2's first series of flights was Bruce J. Hinds (left), chief test pilot for Northrop's B-2 Division, and USAF Col. Richard S. Couch. *(Northrop Grumman)*

of aircraft, including the B-52, B-57, U-2, E-3, E-4, and others. From 1967 to 1982 he served at Edwards AFB and has extensive management and flight experience in all phases of test and operations. Mr. Hinds was born May 8, 1939, in Sioux City, Iowa.

Col. Couch was born July 30, 1946, in Hamilton, Ontario, Canada. He became director of the B-2 Combined Test Force (CTF) at Edwards AFB in June 1985. He is a command pilot with more than 4,600 flying hours in 38 different types of aircraft.

As had been previously programmed by the CTF, the initial flight was intended to assess the B-2's basic flying qualities, especially since it was the world's first all-flying wing bomber (the XB-35/YB-49/YRB-49A aircraft were semi-flying wings). Its design had been thoroughly evaluated during thousands of hours of wind tunnel tests, and its digital fly-by-wire flight control system had been tested and retested. Northrop and the USAF had to know exactly how it was going to fly without any conventional horizontal or vertical tails.

On July 17, 1989, at 6:37 a.m. Pacific Time, Bruce Hinds rotated the aircraft, and the first B-2 lifted off Runway 04 at Palmdale Regional Airport within the USAF Plant 42 complex for its first flight. Boomerang-shaped, it had been some 38 years since a Northrop Flying Wing had flown in the skies over California. *(USAF)*

Lift-off! The first of 21 B-2s climbs up and away from Palmdale to perform its first flight. The flight was successful, and at 8:29 a.m., it made a picture-perfect touchdown at Edwards AFB some 30 mi north of Palmdale. It has now returned to Palmdale, where it is undergoing its Block 30 modifications to become the twenty-first and last operational B-2. *(Northrop Grumman)*

During the B-2's maiden flight, which lasted slightly more than 2 hr, the landing gear remained extended, as had been preplanned. Its maximum speed was 180 kn, maximum altitude was 10,000 ft, and it performed numerous handling qualities tests during the flight. In this view, B-2 number one flies straight at level at 10,000 ft near Edwards AFB. *(USAF)*

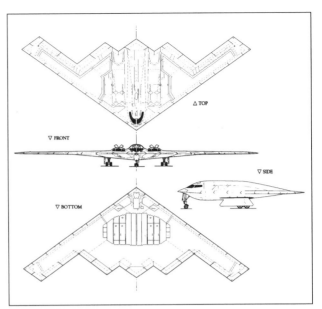

This detailed four-view drawing of the B-2A Spirit shows off its rounded and compound curved lines, as well as its angled and saw-toothed features. The vast array of centrally placed doors shown on the bottom view cover the two main landing gears (outer), the two weapons bays (inner), and the four F118 engines (between the weapons bays and the landing gears). The 16-segment leading edge, 11-segment trailing edge (nine movable, two fixed), and 4-segment wing tip arrangement is noteworthy. *(Northrop Grumman)*

As planned, the B-2's landing gear remained down and locked during the 2-hr and 12-min flight. As the all-wing aircraft climbed to a maximum altitude of 10,000 ft, it reached a maximum speed of 190 kt and performed a series of functional checks of its basic systems. Everything went well.

Then at 8:29 a.m., after a long and slow approach, the crew brought the unique airplane in for a perfect landing on the 15,000-ft Runway 22 at Edwards AFB, California. After the

At first glance, the leading edge of the B-2 flying wing appears to be completely straight. Upon closer inspection, one can notice a series of very slight in-and-out curvatures, which contribute to its stealthy qualities. Noteworthy is the aircraft's "double W" trailing edge planform. *(AFFTC Public Affairs)*

The Edwards AFB North Base complex is shown at the lower right of a B-2 flying over parts of Rogers (center) and Rosamond (upper right) dry lake beds. *(AFFTC Public Affairs)*

Its landing gear down and locked, split drag rudder/airbrake panels opened, and its GLAS, or "beaver tail," deflected downward, the first of 21 B-2As is prepared for landing. This airplane is undergoing Block 30 status modification and will be the last Spirit delivered to the 509th BW. *(AFFTC Public Affairs)*

B-2A number six (AV-6; 82-1071) flies over the NASA complex at the Edwards AFB South Base area, circa 1993. It was named Spirit of MISSISSIPPI on May 23, 1998, and was the nineteenth B-2A delivered to the 509th BW. *(AFFTC Public Affairs)*

This unique illustration shows how America's first jet-powered airplane—the Bell P-59 Airacomet—ultimately metamorphosed into the B-2 flying wing bomber of today. This 50-something year transition includes the Bell X-1 and the Boeing (formerly McDonnell Douglas) F-15E Eagle dual-role strike fighter, all tested at Edwards AFB. *(AFFTC Public Affairs)*

As it flies near Edwards AFB, in this view AV-6 clearly shows off its inward- and outward-curving wing leading edges. Although it is a very large airplane, the RCS of a B-2 is reportedly no bigger than that of a bumblebee. *(Northrop Grumman)*

They say a picture is worth a thousand words. They may be right. When the DoD finally disclosed the actual existence of a stealth fighter on November 10, 1988, the premier B-2 was being prepared for its November 22, 1988, rollout ceremony. Some six years later, during this rare occurrence in 1994, B-2 number six leads a flight of two F-117A Nighthawks. In this view, Lockheed Martin's and Northrop Grumman's different approaches to the creation of viable stealth aircraft is crystal clear. *(Northrop Grumman)*

flight, following a lengthy and detailed inspection of all aircraft systems that lasted nearly a month, the aircraft was cleared for its next journey into the skies above southern California. It and its four F118 engines had performed remarkably well. It was time to see what she could really do.

Flight Testing and Systems Evaluations

"The B-2 also represents strategic stability. They are too slow to be used as first strike weapons but can render the other side's first strike as suicidal. That's why both sides in START have agreed to use counting rules that increase the importance of bombers over missiles. The B-2 program is central to our strategic arms reduction strategy."

—GENERAL JOHN T. CHAIN JR.,
COMMANDER IN CHIEF, STRATEGIC AIR COMMAND,
AND DIRECTOR, STRATEGIC TARGET PLANNING,
MARCH 6, 1990

On August 16, 1989, with its successful first flight accomplished, B-2 number one departed the Air Force Flight Test Center (AFFTC) at Edwards for its second test hop. During this flight, unfortunately, there were some minor concerns with one the engine's oil pressure indicators. Each engine has an accessory drive unit. One of the four drives showed a low oil-pressure reading. It was decided to terminate the flight, a prudent procedure in any type of flight. During the flight, however, the landing gear was retracted and extended for landing and some envelope expansion work was done with the gear up. Bruce Hinds and Col. Couch were again at the controls.

On August 28, 1989, 12 days later, flight number three was completed. That flight lasted 4 hr, 36 min. With Hinds and Couch in command, B-2 number one reached a maximum speed of 300 kt indicated and an altitude of 25,000 ft. The primary mission objectives were expansion of its performance envelope and systems evaluations.

The fourth flight of Air Vehicle 1 (AV-1) occurred on September 21, 1989. It was again operated by Hinds and Couch, and the flight lasted 2 hr, 53 min. During the flight, in preparation for in-flight refueling tests, the aircraft conducted refueling proximity tests with a McDonnell Douglas (now Boeing) KC-10A Extender. It flew a refueling mission without actually hooking up to the tanker's refueling boom. It was a successful flight, with all of the primary mission objectives being made.

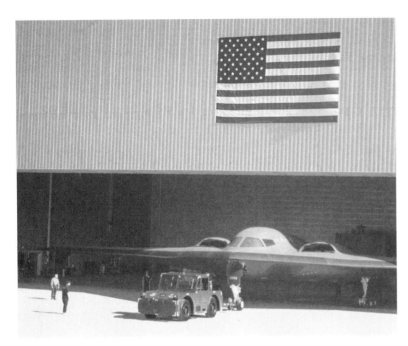

(a)

(b)

(a) B-2 at hangar. (b) Northrop President and CEO Thomas V. "TV" Jones appropriately said during the B-2's November 22, 1988, rollout: "Jack Northrop, we salute you." During the ceremony, Mr. Jones was accompanied by Secretary of the Air Force Edward C. Aldridge Jr., Air Force Chief of Staff Gen. Larry D. Welch, and B-2 Program Manager Brig. Gen. Richard Scofield. *(Northrop Grumman)*

Irving T. "Irv" Waaland, chief designer, Northrop Corporation, and conceptual designer for the B-2 stealth bomber. Instead of using Lockheed's approach of absorbing and deflecting radar signals, Mr. Waaland and other Northrop designers configured their models to bend and defuse them as well. *(Northrop Grumman)*

John Cashen, "Dr. Stealth," along with Irv Waaland, "Mr. B-2," are credited with "fathering" the flying wing concept that evolved into the B-2 of today. Mr. Cashen was responsible for low-observables design, while Mr. Waaland was chief of aerodynamics. *(Northrop Grumman)*

With the Spirit of CALIFORNIA (88-0330) in the background, these two B-2As await their respective Block 30 status upgrades at Palmdale. The four circles are the four ventral air data flow sensors on the starboard wing. There are four more mounted atop the starboard wing, as well as eight more (four ventral, four dorsal) on the port wing. *(Northrop Grumman)*

B-2 Flight Validation Program Highlights

Six full-scale development (FSD) B-2As have been used to conduct the flight validation program at the Air Force Flight Test Center, Edwards AFB, California. The flight-test program was completed on June 30, 1997. Additional testing to confirm the aircraft's Block 30, or full operational configuration, was completed in March 1998.

Between July 17, 1989, and June 30, 1997, the six FSD B-2s (AV-1 through AV-6) logged 5,341 flying hours in 1,148 flights. The B-2 completed Block 1 testing, verifying its basic flight worthiness, in June 1990; this was certified by the U.S. General Accounting Office. Secretary of Defense Richard B. Cheney certified in March 1991 that early Block 2 testing, which included flying qualities and performance evaluations, were satisfactory—without any significant technical or operational difficulties. Testing confirmed the fundamental soundness of the B-2A's low-observable design, a conclusion certified by the Defense Science Board and the Operational Test and Evaluation (OT&E) community.

The premier B-2 (AV-1, or 82-1066) completed its development test program in March 1992. It was extensively used during the testing program for radar cross section (RCS) evaluations and was the initial flight-test aircraft used for envelope expansion, nighttime flying, and nighttime refueling. It was placed in flyable storage until its Block 30 upgrade to become the twenty-first

The sixth of six FSD B-2As and the third of five FSD F-117As flew together near Edwards AFB in 1994. While the B-2 is an all-flying wing, the F-117 is essentially a semi-flying wing. Rumored but undocumented, Lockheed/Rockwell had offered a scaled-up version of the F-117 as their ATB proposal. *(Northrop Grumman)*

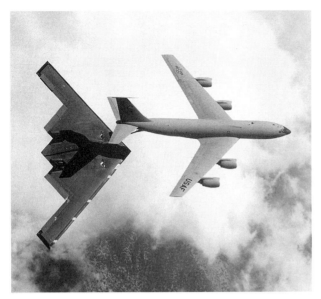

The B-2's four F118 turbofan engines burn a specially blended jet petroleum fuel designated JP-8. Shown here servicing B-2 number four is a Boeing KC-135R Stratotanker. With in-flight refueling, a B-2's range is more than 10,000 mi. *(Northrop Grumman)*

and last operational B-2A. General Richard E. Hawley, Air Combat Command commander, has suggested that it be should be named the Spirit of AMERICA (pending).

After making its first flight on October 19, 1990, the heavily instrumented AV-2 (82-1067) served as the structural flying loads test aircraft, in addition to performance and weapons carriage testing and additional envelope expansion. In March 1998, after its upgrade to operational quality and being named the Spirit of ARIZONA, it joined the fleet at Whiteman AFB, Missouri, as the eighteenth operational B-2A.

The first B-2 with a full complement of radar, navigation, defensive, and offensive avionics equipment was AV-3 (82-1068); it made its first flight on June 18, 1991. After its refurbishment, it was named the Spirit of NEW YORK and joined the 509th BW as the sixteenth operational B-2A in October 1997.

On April 17, 1992, the fourth FSD B-2 (82-1069) made its first flight. It was the armament and avionics test bed, and after its Block 30 modification, it was subsequently named the Spirit of (pending). It became the 509th BW's twentieth operational B-2A; it was delivered to Whiteman AFB in (pending) 1998.

Air Vehicle 5 (82-1070) had its maiden flight on October 5, 1992. It was used in armament and climatic and stealth testing. After it was refurbished, it was named the Spirit of OHIO and became the fourteenth operational B-2A at Whiteman AFB.

An excellent view of the Spirit of WASHINGTON (88-0332), circa 1995. This Spirit, named on October 29, 1994, became the 509th BW's fourth operational B-2A. The "walk here only" within these parallel lines is noteworthy. *(Boeing)*

With the awesome Aurora Borealis overhead, B-2A number five (82-1070) sits on the ramp at Eielson AFB, Alaska, in March, 1996, during Exercise Frozen Spirit 96. The same aircraft had already undergone two months of high-temperature testing at Eglin AFB, Florida, earning the name Fire and Ice. *(USAF)*

A B-2 lifts off just before the 6,000-ft marker at Palmdale. Once airborne, if so required, a B-2 can fly to any given point on Earth with only one aerial refueling to unleash either 40,000 lb of conventional bombs or 25,000 lb of nuclear devices. *(USAF)*

The twenty-first and last B-2A Spirit (93-1088) rolls out of its final assembly area. It was named Spirit of LOUISIANA on November 10, 1997, and was delivered to the 509th as a Block 30 status aircraft. *(USAF)*

What's the very best bomber in the whole wide world actually worth? How about an incredible sum of $2.14 billion each. In April 1997, according to the DoD, the total cost of the B-2 program was announced to be $45 billion. Divide 21 aircraft into $45 billion and the answer is $2.14 billion. *(Northrop Grumman)*

As a B-2 comes up for a drink of JP-8 from a tanker's "flying boom," its opened in-flight refueling receptacle stands ready atop its center wing assembly. After the aircraft is refueled, the receptacle rotates 180° to make the aircraft's dorsal spine stealthy again. *(USAF)*

The last FSD B-2 was AV-6 (82-1071). First flown on February 2, 1993, it was used for avionics and weapons tests. In May 1998, after being named the Spirit of MISSISSIPPI, it joined the 509th BW fleet as the nineteenth operational B-2A.

The B-2's extensive eight-year flight-test program demonstrated and validated aircraft performance, reliability, and system maturity. Testing extended the Spirit to its full flight envelope, with altitudes and speeds up to 100 percent of those expected under operational conditions. The B-2 was thoroughly evaluated over its full operational speed range from lowest to highest Mach number speeds, and from sea level to service ceiling.

Aircraft flutter tests were successfully completed, and the B-2 was deemed flutter-free throughout its entire operational envelope. Flutter, or airflow-induced resonance, is one of the most dangerous reactions an aircraft can experience in flight. This certification, for such an advanced design as the B-2, was a significant milestone. Additionally, in an amazing first, no fuel tank leaks occurred during any portion of the testing program—another significant accomplishment for such a complex and large aircraft with integral, internal body-cavity fuel tanks.

B-2 Spirits successfully released both B-61 and B-83 nuclear bombs, along with Mk-84 conventional bomb shapes, from their rotary launchers. These very first weapon separation tests demonstrated safe and satisfactory releases of these weapons, and indicated that the aircraft design and aerodynamic airflow are suitable for both conventional and nuclear bombardment missions. Follow-on testing was conducted to verify the operational suitability throughout the B-2 flight regime.

Backlighted by the sun, a B-2 makes a low-level high-speed pass at Nellis AFB, Nevada. The B-2, with a full load of weapons, can penetrate enemy territory at just 200 ft above ground level at a speed of Mn 0.95. *(USAF)*

Weapons bay-door testing for destructive acoustic vibrations (when doors are opened at high speed) was successfully completed. A B-2 has two weapons bays and each bay has two doors. This was a critical requirement to ensure that a B-2 is capable of safely performing its weapons-delivery role without destructive vibration.

Other flight tests demonstrated superb integration of the B-2's critical navigation and radar systems. This is a substantial development program that began in January 1987, when navigation and radar tests of the B-2 systems were performed on board a highly modified C-135 Stratolifter aircraft, known as the flight-test avionics laboratory (FTAL). These early development efforts paved the way toward the B-2's well-integrated avionics system.

Flight testing also encompassed 100 percent of the B-2's in-flight air refueling envelope with both KC-10 Extenders and KC-135 Stratotankers—the USAF's two aerial tankers. B-2 pilots say the aircraft is stable and easy to handle and refuel. Other flight-test accomplishments included nighttime aerial refueling and landing tests, which confirmed the B-2's capability to respond to around-the-world and around-the-clock crises and to operate and refuel at night.

The USAF's three strategic bombers, the B-2A, B-52H, and B-1B, from top to bottom, fly together for the first time over the Sierra Nevada mountain range of southern California in September 1994. Vastly different in both their appearances and radar cross sections, they each have the same purpose for being: heavy bombardment. *(Boeing)*

Terrain-following radar (TFR) sensor flight development began in November 1992, using both B-2 and the C-135 FTAL aircraft. Testing at Edwards AFB has demonstrated reliable and fail-safe terrain following at altitudes down to 200 ft over all types of terrain, including water and severe mountainous terrain.

Flight test was just one part of the total B-2 FSD program. Another was the highly successful structural test program. Two test articles—a durability and a static, essentially B-2 airframes without internal components—have demonstrated the strength and durability of the stealth bomber aircraft.

The durability test article completed two *lifetimes* of fatigue testing, which simulated 20,000 hr of flying, or about 30 years of operational use. The static test article testing certified that the B-2 airframe will safely take 150 percent of the operational load and in-flight stress that the aircraft will endure in operational service. The test article was then intentionally taken to its actual breaking point (161 percent!) in a test of ultimate strength.

In December 1993, FSD B-2 number five (AV-5) completed a rigorous six-month program at the Climatic Testing Laboratory at Eglin AFB, Florida. It was then flown to Eielson AFB, Alaska, to undergo cold climate testing. Due to its hot and cold climate testing activities, it was nicknamed "Fire and Ice." It later became the fourteenth operational B-2A Spirit.

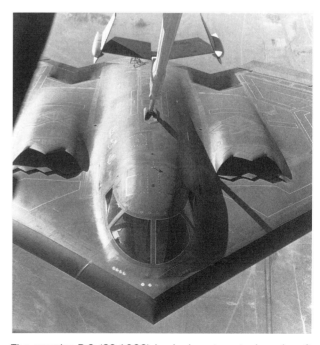

The premier B-2 (82-1066) hooked up to a tanker aircraft for the first time during its sixth flight on November 8, 1989. The aircraft's engine air inlets and exhaust cooling air openings are noteworthy. *(Northrop Grumman)*

Like all of us, the B-2's purpose in life is to survive. In the B-2's case, this is accomplished by defeating the most advanced radar systems known to humanity. This photograph, taken in 1994, shows a B-2 successfully flying against a very sophisticated radar network. *(USAF)*

With a span of 172 ft (52.4 m) and a length of 69 ft (21 m), the B-2's wing area comes in at a whopping 5,140 sq ft (477.5 sq m). Its internal fuel capacity is 180,000 lb (81,635 kg) of JP-8 fuel. *(USAF)*

Some of the highlights of the B-2's flight validation program include:

Longest flight up to May 1998: 16.9 hours, April 25, 1996

Most flights in one week: Nine, from August 15 to 19, 1994

Most flights in one week by a single aircraft: Four, by AV-5, week of July 17, 1995

First cross-country flight: June 5, 1991

First nighttime flight: June 5, 1992

First nighttime aerial refueling flight: July 2, 1992

First drop of an inert (nonexploding) bomb: September 3, 1992

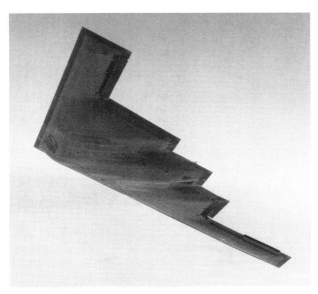

With its landing gear retracted for the first time, the first of 21 B-2s is shown here on its second flight at Edwards AFB. *(Northrop Grumman)*

B-2 Program Awards

As of this writing, the B-2 program awards include:

- *The Collier Trophy*—The prestigious aviation award presented annually by the National Aeronautic Association was presented in May 1992 to "The Northrop Grumman Corporation, The Industry Team, and the United States Air Force for the design, development, production, and flight testing of the B-2 aircraft, which has contributed significantly to America's enduring leadership in aerospace and the country's future national security."

- *Theodore von Karman Award*—The Air Force Association awarded the B-2 test team this prestigious award in September 1990 for the most outstanding contribution in the field of science and engineering.

Also in September 1990, the pilots who first flew the B-2 received one of the test pilot community's highest awards. Bruce Hinds, then Northrop Grumman's chief test pilot, and USAF Col. Rick Couch were given the Society of Experimental Test Pilots' Iven C. Kincheloe Award for outstanding performance in flight testing.

B-2 Manufacturing Breakthroughs

The Northrop Grumman B-2A Spirit is not only advanced in design, mission, and performance, but also in materials inventiveness, fabrication, and fabrication processes. According to Northrop Grumman, the B-2 industrial team developed almost 900 new materials and processes to manufacture this revolutionary bomber.

Northrop Grumman's two-dimensional and three-dimensional (2D/3D) electronic product definition computer system is possibly the most momentous manufacturing feat of the B-2 program. The complete character of the B-2 aircraft is maintained on computer in easy-to-understand, three-dimensional graphics. These can record measurements accurate in billionths of an inch and allow airframe tolerances to be measured in ten-thousandths of an inch over the entire length, height, and width of a large aircraft—the very kind of accuracy needed to achieve the B-2's low-observable characteristics.

All of the major subcontractors and the USAF are tied into the system, ensuring that participating B-2 team members have the same up-to-date information. Logistics, maintenance, and support organizations use the system, and computerized support information is in place at the Spirit's maintenance headquarters at the USAF's Oklahoma City Air Logistics Center at Tinker AFB. Licensing agreements that allow companies to use the 2D/3D system on commercial or military aircraft/spacecraft projects were signed into place at major B-2 subcontractors Boeing and Vought Aircraft.

B-2 manufacturing requirements led to the development of a high-speed milling machine that reduces processing time and increases quality. It was developed by Hughes Aircraft Company's Radar Systems Group (now part of Raytheon), a member of the B-2 industrial team. The computer-driven machine's spindle operates at speeds up to 100,000 revolutions per minute (rpm), compared to standard spindle rates of 20,000 to 30,000 rpm for high-speed milling or routing. Use of this advanced milling machine resulted in B-2 components being planed (milled or cut) or grooved (routed) 20 times faster and to tighter tolerances than ever before. Fischer North American manufactures the spindles for the machine.

A computer-controlled drill marketed by the Cooper Power Tool Division of Cooper Industries that was developed for the B-2 program greatly improves quality and reduces costs. The Adaptive Control Drilling System, or ACDS, senses the hardness of different materials such as aluminum alloys, titanium alloys, and graphite composite materials, adjusts drill bit speed accordingly, and automatically retracts periodically to allow cuttings (metallic alloys or composite materials shavings) to be removed from drill holes. The result is an improvement of the quality of drilled holes and a reduction of costly rework. Average drilling time for a hole through such layers is reduced by one-half. Besides speeding production, this extends an expensive drill bit's operating life. Drill bits that had to be resharpened after every 15 holes now can be used to drill 60 holes before resharpening is required.

A machine developed for Northrop Grumman can cut composite material into required shapes three times faster and with much greater precision than traditional composite cutters. This next-generation ultrasonic cutting machine, with improved positioning accuracy and cutting speeds, is marketed by American GFM. The machine uses ultrasonic energy to process materials at a rate of 1,200 in/min with positioning accuracy to within plus-or-minus .010 in (compared with 400 in/min and plus-or-minus .032 in for conventional cutters).

New automated methods and machines for fabricating composite components, including some of the largest primary composite structures ever made, are now in use. The machinery includes equipment for fabrication of structural rib stiffeners that reduces hand labor by 69 percent and improves quality and reduces scrap material. Software includes packages that allow application of composite tape to large, contoured components. This machinery and software is being marketed by Cincinnati Milacron and Ingersoll Milling Machine.

Many of these developments have been and continue to be transferred to other sectors of U.S. industry. Northrop Grumman and other B-2 team members have given technical presentations throughout the United States to organizations such as the Society of Manufacturing Engineers, the Society of Automotive Engineers, the Aerospace Industries Association, and the Society for the Advancement of Materials and Process Engineering. In addition, equipment developed for the B-2 program is available to American commercial manufacturers.

Since the overall success of the B-2 as an operational stealth bomber required such a multitude of production breakthroughs, it generated many new manufacturing devices and techniques.

The B-2 Nationwide Industrial Team

The USAF's B-2 program is supported nationwide by tens of thousands of men and women at prime contractor Northrop Grumman, key subcontractors Boeing, General Electric and Hughes, and other suppliers and subcontractors in 46 states and the District of Columbia. The states with the largest number of suppliers include Arizona, California, Colorado, Connecticut, Florida, Georgia, Idaho, Illinois, Iowa, Kansas, Kentucky, Maryland, Massachusetts, Michigan, Minnesota, New Hampshire, New Jersey, New Mexico, New York, Ohio, Oklahoma, Texas, Utah, Vermont, Virginia, and Washington.

The United States' current—and probably last—fleet of heavy bombardment aircraft is comprised of the venerable Boeing B-52H Stratofortress (above), Boeing North American B-1B Lancer (center), and Northrop Grumman B-2A Spirit. Respectively, the number of each type in operational USAF inventory is about 90 each for the B-52H and B-1B, and 20 for the B-2A. At this writing, the last of 21 B-2As (tentatively named Spirit of AMERICA) is scheduled to be delivered in early 1999. *(USAF)*

Just before the first B-2's public debut on November 22, 1988, the USAF released this artist rendition of what the aircraft would look like. Except for the noticeable lack of detail on the aircraft's engine exhaust nozzles, the illustration was essentially right on. *(USAF)*

At this writing, General Electric has only been allowed to release this photograph of the nonafterburning F118-GE-100 turbofan engine. Rated at 17,300 lb (7,847 kg) thrust each, four of these engines provide a total thrust output of 69,200 lb (31,388 kg) for the B-2A. This is enough to propel it to a maximum speed of Mn 0.95, or nine and one-half tenths the speed of sound. *(General Electric)*

The "dashboard" in B-2A number one, circa 1989, illustrates a number of cathode ray tubes, or CRTs, between-the-legs flight-control sticks à la a fighter, and numerous buttons, dials, and switches. The left-hand engine throttle quadrant for the right-hand seat (the left seat's throttles are out of view) is noteworthy. *(Northrop Grumman)*

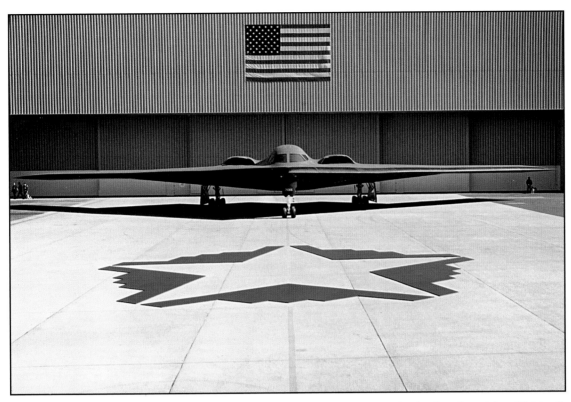

Dateline: November 22, 1988. The premier B-2A Spirit appears to the public for the first time at its official roll-out ceremony at U.S. Air Force Plant 42 in Palmdale, California. Just as the world was beginning to get used to the multifaceted stealth fighter's strange appearance, the stealth bomber's curvaceous lines came into focus. Two very different philosophies on stealth had led the way to two very different trains of thought on how to create stealth aircraft. *(Northrop Grumman Corporation)*

The first of 21 B-2 air vehicles (AV-1) rose off the Antelope Valley floor to commit itself to flight for the very first time on July 17, 1989. With Bruce Hinds in the left seat and Col. Rick Couch to his right, the unique aircraft took off at 6:37 a.m. PDT and landed at 8:29 a.m. PDT. According to post-flight reports, the 1-hr, 52-min flight was completely successful. After nearly 40 years, a flying wing aircraft had returned to the skies. *(Northrop Grumman Corporation)*

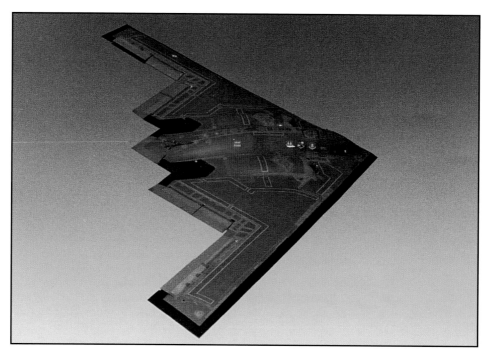

Although the B-2 is not capable of supersonic flight, it has a slippery aerodynamic configuration. Neither the F-117 stealth fighter nor the B-2 stealth bomber has afterburning engines; thus, they are only capable of high subsonic speeds. *(Northrop Grumman Corporation)*

B-2 number one banks right during a test hop out of Edwards in late 1989. The fact that it has no vertical tail surfaces whatsoever is obvious in this view. In other words, it is a pure all-flying wing aircraft—Jack Northrop's ultimate goal. *(Northrop Grumman Corporation)*

Beginning in late 1947, in hope of producing a number of jet-powered flying wing bombers for the USAF, Northrop initiated flight tests on two 8-jet YB-49s. A semi-flying wing configuration—note vertical tails—the aircraft proved too unstable as an accurate bombardment platform. *(AFFTC/HO)*

The fifth B-2A (AV-5) sits under a nearly full moon at Eielson AFB in Alaska in the summer of 1996, where it underwent successful cold-climate testing. All new types of combat aircraft must successfully complete a series of cold-climate tests before they can become operational. It was no different for stealthy Spirit aircraft. *(The Boeing Company)*

Showing its relatively deep V-shaped underbelly, the third B-2A (AV-3) was displayed during an open house in the summer of 1991, whereby those in attendance could get a much better look at the USAF's stealth bomber. The aircraft's very wide stance is noteworthy. *(Photograph by Tony Landis)*

At only 69 ft (20.9 m) in length and 17 ft (5.1 m) in height, the large size of the B-2 is not readily apparent in this view of B-2 number seven (AV-7). Yet with its 172-ft (52.12-m) wingspan, it is a very large aircraft. *(Northrop Grumman Corporation)*

After its delivery flight from California, B-2A number eight (AV-8) rolls to a stop at Whiteman AFB on December 17, 1993. Named the Spirit of MISSOURI, this became the first operational B-2A on this date. Exactly 90 years earlier, the Wright Brothers made the world's first controlled and powered aircraft flight in history. *(USAF)*

The two side-by-side weapons bays in each B-2 feature large-volume capacities, as shown here while 509th BW ordnance technicians load a weapon into one of these bays on a Spirit aircraft. In full battle dress, a single B-2 can carry 40,000 lb (18,144 kg) of conventional or nuclear weapons. That is 20 tons of ordnance, or about the combined gross takeoff weight of four P-51D Mustangs of WW II *(USAF)*

The actual size of a B-2A can be realized in this close-up view of the Spirit of Florida (92-0700) in a 509th BW hangar at Whiteman AFB in late 1996. With its typical takeoff weight of 336,500 lb (152,635 kg), a single B-2 weighs more than five fully loaded B-17G Flying Fortresses of WW II. *(USAF)*

Perched high above the clouds during a training mission out of Whiteman AFB in the fall of 1998, this B-2 offers up an excellent view of what an all-flying wing aircraft should look like. Powered by four General Electric F118-GE-100 turbofan engines (without an aerial refueling), a B-2's maximum range is about 6,000 nmi (9,600 km). *(USAF)*

Structures and Systems

"Remember the Libyan raid? If we had had the B-2,
three or four B-2s flying from the United States could
have done it . . . with complete surprise."

—GENERAL BERNARD RANDOLPH, COMMANDER,

AIR FORCE SYSTEMS COMMAND,

29 APRIL 1989

T he Northrop Grumman B-2A Spirit stealth bomber is a relatively large and heavy aircraft. It is much bigger and heavier than it actually looks due to its all-flying wing configuration. Yet, since it is an extremely complex weapon system, its structures are elaborate and its systems are numerous.

Manufacturing Processes

The B-2's manufacturing processes are far too many to name in the space allowed. Basically, the 21 production B-2A Spirit aircraft came together as follows:

1. The left and right intermediate wing assemblies were joined to the aft/center wing assembly.

2. The left and right outboard wing assemblies were attached to the left and right intermediate wing assemblies.

3. The crew station assembly was attached to the aft/center wing assembly.

4. The nose and main landing gear units were attached.

5. The left and right wing tips were attached to the left and right outboard wing assemblies.

6. The centrally mounted nose-piece assembly was attached to the crew station assembly and the 14 wing leading edge segments (seven left/seven right) were attached to the crew station assembly, intermediate wing assembly, and the outboard wing assemblies.

7. The left and right fixed trailing edges were attached to the left and right intermediate wing assemblies; the Gust Load Alleviation System (GLAS) assembly was attached to the aft/center wing assembly.

8. The left and right split rudders were attached to the left and right outboard wing assemblies' trailing edges.

9. The left and right sets of inboard, middle, and outboard elevons were attached to the trailing edges of the outboard wing assemblies and the intermediate wing assemblies.

10. The left and right radar system assemblies were attached to the crew station assembly.

11. The four F118 engines, air inlet ducts, and exhaust ducts and nozzles were installed.

The above aircraft assembly steps are simplified, but they provide a general view on how each B-2 airplane came together during their manufacturing processes.

The prime contractor, responsible for overall system design and integration, is Northrop Grumman's B-2 Division. Boeing Military Airplanes Company (BMAC), Hughes Radar Systems Group (HRSG), and General Electric Aircraft Engines (GEAE) are key members of the aircraft contractor team. Another major contractor, responsible for crewperson training devices (weapon system trainer and mission trainer) is Hughes Training Incorporated (HTI)—Link Division, formerly known as C.A.E.—Link Flight Simulator Corporation. Northrop Grumman and its major subcontractor HTI, excluding Link Division, is responsible for developing and integrating all crewperson and maintenance training programs. A former major member of the contractor team was Vought Aircraft Corporation, now part of Northrop Grumman.

Primary maintenance responsibility for the B-2 weapon system is divided between Oklahoma City Air Logistics Center at Tinker AFB, Oklahoma, for avionics software (contractor); Ogden Air Logistics Center, Hill AFB, Utah, for landing gear and trainers (contractor); and

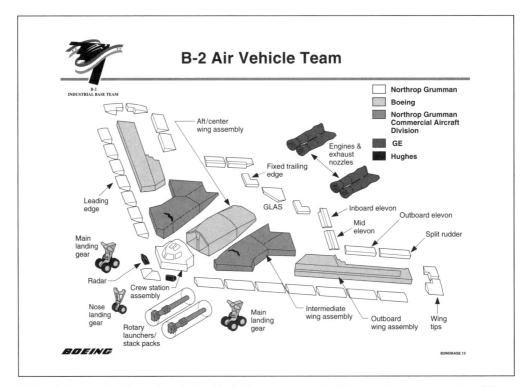

Although thousands of suppliers helped build the USAF's fleet of B-2s, only a small number of them actually provided the main sections for their assembly processes. As shown here in this exploded view, Northrop Grumman provided the radar covers, crew station assemblies, leading edges, wing tips, and both the fixed and movable trailing edges; Northrop Grumman's Commercial Aircraft Division (formerly Vought Aircraft) supplied the intermediate wing assemblies; Hughes Aircraft provided the radar sets; General Electric built the engines; and Boeing delivered the nose and main landing gear assemblies, outboard wings, rotary launchers and stack packs, and the aft-center wing assemblies. *(The Boeing Company)*

A large structural section of a B-2 (an outboard wing) is seen here during production at Boeing's Defense and Space Group, Military Airplanes Division, in Seattle, Washington. *(The Boeing Company)*

A Boeing employee is assisting in the automated fabrication process for advanced composite structural components the company supplied for the B-2 bomber. The actual buildup of composite materials is accomplished by an automated tape-laying machine seen in the background. *(The Boeing Company)*

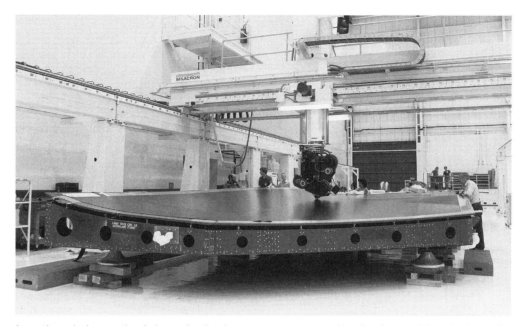

An outboard wing section is in production here, as an automated laminating machine, designed for contour surfaces, is laying down fabric-like composite tape, which is layered to form the parts. The parts are then cured in Boeing's autoclave—the world's largest. *(The Boeing Company)*

The inside of a Boeing-built outboard wing section. Believed to be the world's largest advanced-composite component, it was fabricated using the latest in automated equipment and manufacturing techniques. *(The Boeing Company)*

A Boeing worker works on a left, outboard wing section. Boeing manufactured and delivered 42 outboard wing sections: 21 left, 21 right. *(The Boeing Company)*

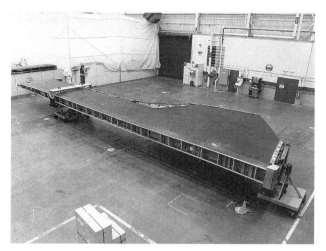

Another view of a nearly complete outboard wing section—a right one, this time. This one, as a matter of fact, was for the twenty-first and last B-2 to be built; it was delivered to Northrop Grumman in May 1994. *(The Boeing Company)*

The final B-2 aft-center wing section (at right), number 21, is shown here under construction. The day this photo was taken, August 12, 1993, portions of the B-2's hydraulics and electronics were being installed; it was delivered in December 1993. *(The Boeing Company)*

the Northrop Grumman Site 4 facility at Air Force Plant 42 at Palmdale for periodic depot maintenance and Block upgrades (Figs. 6-9, 6-10, and 6-11).

General Electric F118-GE-100 Turbofan Engine

According to an official USAF fact sheet, the B-2A Spirit is powered by four General Electric F118-GE-100 nonafterburning 17,300-lb (7,847-kg) thrust, static-at-sea-level turbofan

This photo was released shortly after B-2 number one rolled out in November 1988. It shows B-2 numbers two, three, and four in various stages of assembly in Palmdale, circa mid-1989, before the first flight of AV-1. *(Northrop Grumman)*

Front-to-back, B-2 aircraft numbers 16 through 21 are shown in various stages of their final assembly processes. Some 45 years earlier, the XB-35 Flying Wing bombers (see Chapter 1) were assembled outside in Hawthorne, California. *(Northrop Grumman)*

A couple of early production B-2s are shown undergoing their respective Block 30 modifications in Palmdale, circa early 1998. Eventually, all B-2s will feature Block 30 capabilities. *(Northrop Grumman)*

engines. Its four powerplants, closely mounted in pairs, are buried deep inside the B-2's structure. Forward of the engine fronts, or faces, atop the aircraft are scalloped air inlets, followed by a sophisticated series of snakelike air ducts, optimized to properly feed the correct ratio of air to their fuel systems. Sitting atop each air inlet/duct assembly are a pair of upward-opening auxiliary air inlets for taxiing and low-speed flying maneuvers. Aft of the engines, atop the aircraft are the engine exhaust channels.

The F118 turbofan engine, derived from General Electric's F101 bomber engine and F110

It takes four 17,300-lb (7,847-kg) thrust engines to power the B-2A Spirit. Therefore, four nonaugmented (afterburning) General Electric F118-GE-100 turbofan engines give each B-2 69,200 lb (31,388 kg) of maximum propulsive thrust. *(General Electric Aircraft Engines)*

fighter engine and measuring 100.5 in (2,553 mm) in length and 46.5 in (1,181 mm) in diameter, has electro-hydromechanical engine controls. The relatively small and light non-afterburning F118 employs new long-chord fan blade technology, resulting in higher thrust, without the need for a larger size and weight. It uses a three-stage fan with variable inlet guide vanes, a one-stage high-pressure turbine, and a two-stage low-pressure turbine. It features an airflow of about 280 lb/sec (127,12 kg/sec) and a bypass ratio of about 0.80:1.

Flight Control System

The B-2's flight control system is comprised of an remarkably mature fly-by-wire (FBW) system and a computerized digital-type, quadruple redundant operating suite for safe flying operations. The B-2's flight control system uses fiber-optic data transmission lines for extra fast and more positive pilot control. The flight controls are operated by fighter-like control sticks mounted directly in front of each one of the aircraft's pilot seats. The two engine throttle quadrants are located to the left on each pilot.

Flying Surfaces

Due to its pure all-flying wing configuration, the B-2's flying surfaces are not only unique, they are also somewhat complicated. All of the B-2's flying surfaces are located at its serrated set of "double W" trailing edges—numbering eight in all. They are comprised of: (1) two sets of combination drag rudders and speed brakes, one on either side, located farthest outboard near the wingtips; (2) two 3-part sets of elevons, one set on either side, located inboard of the drag rudders; and (3) a "beaver tail" assembly, located farthest aft on centerline, which is called the Gust Load Alleviation System (GLAS).

The two drag rudder assemblies, used for turning if deployed independently or as air brakes if extended in unison, are essentially a four-part split-flap system whereby each drag rudder has an upper and a lower appendage. The six elevon flying control surfaces, used together or separately, are used as elevators and/or flaps. Also, the so-called beaver tail assembly, used primarily for pitch control, provides additional stability for extremely accurate (unguided) weapon deliveries (e.g., the dropping of, say, eighty 500-lb conventional free-fall gravity bombs).

Crew Accommodation

Unlike previous heavy bombardment aircraft, having from four (B-1B) to five (B-52H) crew members, the B-2 is operated by only two crew members—the pilot and the mission commander. It has space for a third crew member if needed. Sitting side-by-side on Boeing Advanced Concept Ejection Seats or ACES II zero-altitude/zero-speed ejection seats, the crew operates the aircraft in a fully pressurized cockpit with large-area windscreens for excellent front and side visibility. If emergency ejection is required, panels directly above the crew are jettisoned, and the ACES II seats rocket upward and aft in a predetermined sequence so that neither crew member's ejection interferes with the other.

Directly in front of each pilot is the fighter-like control stick and four multifunction display (MFD) screens. Located directly between them is the center console, which among other equipment, has the right-hand pilot's engine throttle quadrant, navigation and radio equipment, landing gear controls, and so on. The aircraft's two-part electronics (avionics) equipment racks are located directly aft of the two pilots seats. The third seat, if needed, would be located aft of the right-hand avionics rack; a third emergency ejection hatch is directly above that location.

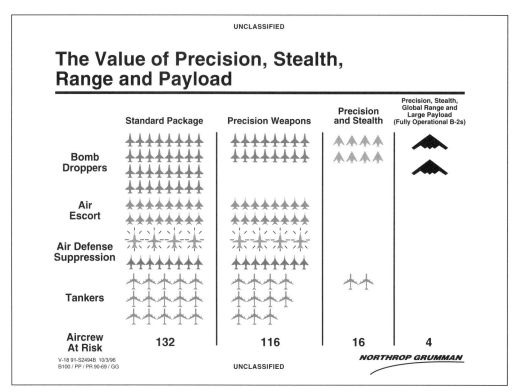

The value of third-generation stealth, precision-strike, global-range, and large weapons payload for fully operational B-2As is illustrated here. In one of these three comparisons, it would take 116 crew members and a standard package of 75 aircraft to accomplish what only two B-2s and their four crew members could achieve on the same mission. The two other scenarios are likewise impressive. *(Northrop Grumman)*

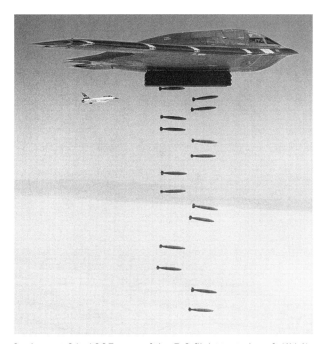

On August 31, 1995, one of the B-2 flight-test aircraft (AV-4), on its one-hundredth flight, conducted a drop of 80 Mk 82 500-lb class warhead bombs over one of Edwards' bombing ranges. Operational B-2s can carry up to 80 of these 500-lb conventional weapons. *(Northrop Grumman)*

The B-2 Weapon System

Having been declared fully operational on April 1, 1997, the B-2A Spirit is a complete weapon system, and with its constantly improving multimission capabilities, it is fully able to perform a multitude of war-fighting scenarios. Whether its twin weapons bays are packed with conventional or nuclear ordnance, it is an awesome war machine.

A B-2 pilot stated in 1995: "The B-2 stealth bomber doesn't have a 'cloaking device' like the galactic battle cruisers in the *Star Trek* television series and movies; it's not invisible to the eye. It does, however, guard its most secret attributes from potential adversaries . . . It can strike without detection . . . In other words, it doesn't have to be seen to fire. This capability was demonstrated by F-117s during the air campaign against Iraq in Operation Desert Storm. Time and time again, the stealth fighters delivered their precision-guided munitions with pinpoint accuracy—and without a scratch. This is also what a B-2 bomber can do, but with 14 more 2,000-lb munitions per sortie."

Within its two weapons bays, which are located inboard of the main landing gear bays on either side of

USAF ordnance personnel upload forty 80 Mk 82 500-lb class warhead bombs onto the two bomb rack assemblies, or BRAs, (20 per rack) in the right weapons bay of the Spirit of PENNSYLVANIA (93-1087); forty other Mk 82s were loaded into the left-side bay. After the 80 Mk 82s were loaded, the aircraft departed for a tiny island in the Farralon Bomb Range in the Pacific Ocean. Flown by Capts. Tony Monetti and Christopher Harness, this was the first operational maximum load of Mk 82s to be dropped by the 509th BW. *(USAF)*

aircraft centerline, each B-2A Spirit can use most weapons in the U.S. arsenal. These weapons include the least sophisticated conventional warhead dumb bomb, the most accurate conventional warhead smart bomb, any type of free-fall or standoff nuclear device such as high-yield thermonuclear bombs, and air-launched cruise missiles with thermonuclear warheads.

The B-2's total payload is at least 40,000 lb (18,144 kg), and it is housed within two large-volume weapons bays that are covered by a set of outward-opening/inward-closing doors. These doors, each one being fully optimized for stealth, or low observability, are made of composite materials and feature saw-tooth, or dog-tooth, leading and trailing edges. For combat operations they are programmed to rapidly open, and after weapons release, rapidly shut. This quick action is designed to reduce the aircraft's RCS as much as possible during combat operations.

Weapons

The primary mission of the Northrop Grumman B-2A Spirit is to enable any theater commander to hold at risk and, if necessary, attack an enemy's war-making potential. Most important are those time-critical targets that, if not destroyed in the first hours or days of a conflict, would allow unacceptable damage to be inflicted on the friendly side. The B-2 is optimized to carry and deliver a wide array of weapons. These include the following:

- Hughes Missile Systems/Boeing AGM-129A ACM
- Boeing GBU-31 JDAM

An inert (nonexplosive) GAM-113 deep-penetrating munition is loaded into a B-2. The GAM-113 integrates a Northrop Grumman–developed inertial guidance tail kit with conventional BLU-113 4,700-lb class warhead bomb bodies to produce all-weather, day-or-night, launch-and-leave, near-precision weapons with circular error probable (CEP) accuracy of 20 ft. *(Northrop Grumman)*

An inert GAM-113 4,700-lb munition is released from a flight-test B-2 (82-1069/AV-4) during a February 1997 test at China Lake Naval Weapons Center in California. Each B-2 can carry up to eight of these deep-penetrating weapons, which are most effective against hard and deeply buried targets. The GAM-113 uses the GPS-Aided Targeting System/ GPS-Aided Munition (GATS/GAM) technology developed by a Northrop Grumman/Hughes Aircraft team to provide the B-2 with a near-precision weapon capability until the 2,000-lb class warhead Joint Direct Attack Munition, or JDAM, becomes operational. *(USAF)*

- GBU-37 "Bunker Buster"
- Lockheed Martin AGM-158 JASSM
- Raytheon/Texas Instruments System AGM-154A JSOW
- Nuclear bombs
- Conventional bombs

Hughes Missile Systems/Boeing AGM-129A ACM

First flown in July 1985, the AGM-129A ACM, or advanced cruise missile, is a subsonic long-range (1,870 mi, approximate) standoff weapon with low-observable, or stealth, characteristics. Originally deployed only on the B-52H and evaluated for use on the B-1B, it has been adopted for use by the B-2A. It has improved range, accuracy, survivability, and target flexibility compared with the Boeing AGM-86B ALCM.

Originally developed by the Convair Division of General Dynamics (now Hughes Missile Systems), the AGM-129A weighs approximately 3,710 lb at launch and is armed with a 200 KT W80-1 thermonuclear warhead. A single B-2 can carry up to 16 ACMs on its two CSLR, or common strategic rotary launchers—one in either weapons bay, and eight ACMs on each one.

The AGM-129A is powered by a single nonafterburning Williams International F112-WR-100 turbofan engine. It is 20 ft, 10 in long and has a 10-ft, 2-in wingspan. It has a body width of 2 ft, 3¾ in. Its guidance unit, updated with TERCOM, or terrain contour matching, is a Litton inertial navigation system.

The last of 461 AGM-129As was delivered in August 1993.

Boeing GBU-31 JDAM

The Boeing (formerly McDonnell Douglas) JDAM, or Joint Direct Attack Munition, is a guidance kit that converts existing unguided free-fall "dumb" bombs into accurately guided "smart" weapons. The JDAM kit consists of a new tail section that contains an inertial navigation system (INS)/Global Positioning System (GPS). Currently for the B-2A, the Mk 83 1,000-lb class warhead, Mk 84 2,000-lb class warhead, BLU-109 2,000-lb class warhead, and BLU-110 1,000-lb class warhead bombs are being modified to make JDAM weapons for the Spirit.

As a growth option for the B-2 and others, 500-lb class Mk 82 bombs are being developed to fit into the JDAM family. At this writing, Boeing was slated to complete this development program by late 1998. With the independent targeting capability of the JDAM, a single

B-2 with eighty 500-lb class JDAM weapons could actually hit 80 different targets, a vast improvement over the traditional carpet bombing mission.

On a combat mission, a single B-2A can carry twelve 2,000-lb class JDAMs—six in either weapons bay. When launched, these weapons have proved to be highly accurate (approximately 6 meters CEP, or circular error probable) and can be delivered in any "flyable" weather. Satellite-guided then, JDAMs can be launched from more than 15 miles from the target, with updates from GPS satellites to help guide the weapon to the target. Additional growth potentially includes extending the range to greater than 35 miles and improving on the high accuracy already provided by the JDAMs GPS/INS.

Boeing delivered 140 early operational capability, or EOC, JDAM kits to the 509th BW at Whiteman AFB in 1997. On June 24, 1998, Boeing delivered the first production JDAM.

GBU-37 "Bunker Buster"

The GBU-37 is a satellite-guided 5,000-lb class conventional warhead weapon optimized to deeply penetrate its target (up to 10 ft of hardened concrete) before exploding.

Lockheed Martin AGM-158 JASSM (proposed for the B-2)

As the replacement for the canceled Northrop AGM-137A Tri-Service Standoff Attack Missile (TSSAM), the AGM-158 Joint Air-to-Surface Standoff Missile (JASSM) is being developed by Lockheed Martin as a stealthy, long-range weapon with a 2,000-lb class conventional warhead. The JASSM is a precision cruise missile designed for launch from outside area defenses to kill hard, medium-hardened, soft, and area-fixed and relocatable targets.

The AGM-158's midcourse guidance is provided by a GPS-aided (Global Positioning System) inertial navigation system (INS) protected by a new high, antijam GPS null steering antenna system. In the terminal phase, the JASSM is guided by an imaging infrared (heat) seeker and a general pattern match-autonomous target recognition system that provides aim-point detection, tracking, and strike. It also offers growth potential for different warheads and seekers, and for extended range.

The AGM-158 JASSM concept uses the Hard Target Smart Fuse (HTSF), an accelerometer-based electronic fuse that allows control of the detonation point by layer counting, distance, or time. The accelerometer senses G loads on the bomb due to deceleration as it penetrates through the target. The fuse can distinguish between earth, concrete, rock, and air.

As originally planned, a B-2 was to carry eight TSSAMs—four in either weapons bay. When they become operational, it is likely that a B-2 will also carry eight JASSMs. However, this remains to be seen.

Raytheon/Texas Instruments Systems AGM-154A JSOW

The B-2 can carry eight AGM-154A JSOW, or joint standoff weapons, which are stealthy glide bombs—four in each weapons bay. The Raytheon/Texas Instruments Systems JSOW is a 2,000-lb class weapon that, depending on the altitude from which it is released, glides some 40 to 60 miles to either unleash submunitions or to dive headfirst into its target with a conventional high-explosive warhead.

The "Jersey Cow," as the JSOW is nicknamed, uses both Global Positioning System (GPS) and inertial navigation system (INS) for its guidance. Its circular error probable (CEP) is approximately 40 ft. The USAF plans to procure more than 12,000 JSOWs, and of these, some 8,000 will be submunition dispenser types, some 2,100 will be of the sensor-fused weapon (SFW) type, and the rest will be armed with unitary (conventional) warheads.

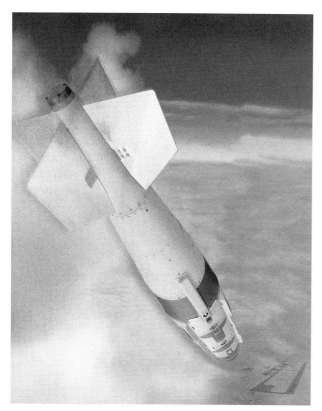

An artist rendering of a 2,000-lb class warhead GBU-31 JDAM. The Boeing-developed JDAM is a low-cost guidance kit that converts existing unguided free-fall Mk 83, Mk 84, BLU-109, and BLU-110 bombs into accurately guided weapons. JDAM weapons can be launched (dropped) more than 15 mi from the target and uses updates from GPS satellites and its inertial navigation system, or INS, to help guide the weapon to the target area. The first production JDAM was delivered on June 24, 1990. *(The Boeing Company)*

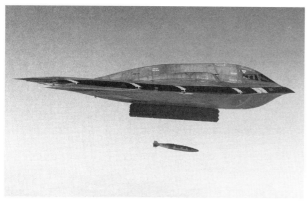

The fourth FSD B-2 (82-1069) drops one of four inert 2,000-lb class JDAM weapons on a White Sands, New Mexico, test range against four deeply buried targets on April 28, 1998. Based upon the BLU-109, this version of the JDAM has a CEP of 13 m. *(The Boeing Company)*

Nuclear Bombs

The B-2 is optimized to carry two different types of nuclear bombs—the B61 and B83. On a nuclear mission, a single B-2 can carry 16 B61-1/-7 10- to 500-kiloton thermonuclear bombs, eight in each weapons bay, on the Boeing Advanced Rotary Launcher (ARL). Another version of the B61, the B61-11, is a deep-penetrating nuclear bomb that explodes only after it has deeply penetrated (up to 20 ft of hardened concrete) an underground target.

In another scenario, on a nuclear mission, a single B-2 can carry 16 B83 1- to 2-megaton thermonuclear bombs, eight in each weapons bay, on Boeing ARLs.

Conventional Bombs

In the conventional role, B-2s are capable of carrying just about anything in the U.S. arsenal's inventory. In practice, these weapons are carried on an Advanced Rotary Launcher (ARL) or a bomb rack assembly (BRA). These conventional high-explosive (HE) warhead weapons include the 500-lb class Mk 82, 750-lb class Mk 117, and 2,000-lb class Mk 84, among many other types of ordnance, including 500-lb class Mk 36 mines. Each B-2 can also carry up to 36 750-lb class Mk 117 bombs or 750-lb class Mk 62 mines—18 in each one of its weapons bays.

Avionics System

The details of the B-2's avionics system are still classified. Generally, though, it is comprised of 13 common avionics control unit (ACU) processors that perform numerous duties. Some of these functions include terrain following/terrain avoidance (TA/TF), defensive and offensive systems management, and navigation.

Landing Gear

The nose and main landing gear assemblies for each one of the 21 B-2 aircraft were provided by Boeing and are comprised of a single two-wheeled nose landing gear and two 4-wheeled main landing gears. Although Boeing had already provided the 21 complete sets of landing gears for the B-2 program, it was subsequently awarded an $80 million contract to upgrade a number of existing sets. These refurbished landing gears are replacement sets for the six flight-test aircraft and others—including the set for the original B-2A (82-1066). The final B-2 landing gear was delivered two months early to Northrop Grumman in Palmdale, California, in June 1998. After the aircraft is refurbished to

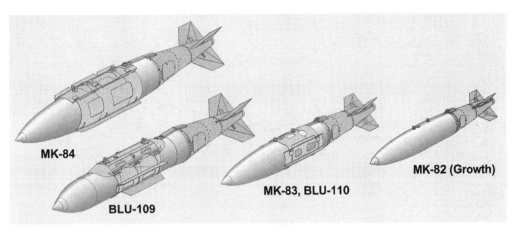

The JDAM family is shown here. The 500-lb class warhead Mk 82 is a Boeing-funded variant of the JDAM whose development was completed in late 1998. *(The Boeing Company)*

Block 30 standard, AV-1 is scheduled to be the twenty-first and last B-2A Spirit to be delivered to the 509th BW at Whiteman AFB in early 2000.

Originally built as a dedicated flight-test vehicle, the first stealth bomber flew 81 test missions before it was placed into extended flyable storage at Palmdale in March 1993. The main landing gear stands 8 ft tall and weighs about 9,500 lb. Goodyear supplied the tires and Allied Signal built the wheels and brakes.

Boeing's delivery of the last refurbished landing gear units marked the completion of its portion of the upgrade program for this first, and now last, B-2.

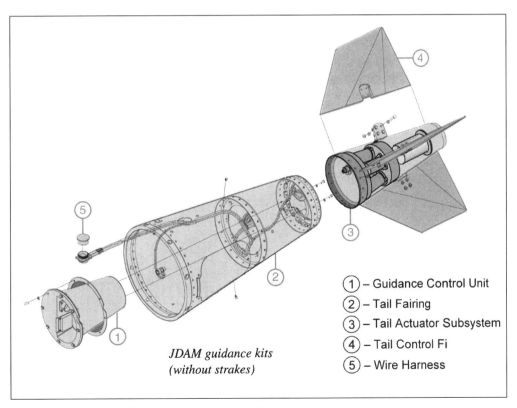

JDAM guidance kits
(without strakes)

1 – Guidance Control Unit
2 – Tail Fairing
3 – Tail Actuator Subsystem
4 – Tail Control Fi
5 – Wire Harness

A JDAM guidance kit (without the mid-body stabilization strakes) is shown in this exploded view. *(The Boeing Company)*

Lockheed Martin Skunk Works is developing the AGM-158 Joint Air-to-Surface Standoff Missile, or JASSM, for use by the B-2 and others. As the replacement for the canceled AGM-137 Tri-Service Standoff Attack Missile, the JASSM is to be a very stealthy, long-range 2,000-lb class warhead weapon, capable of high-accuracy strikes. Here a JASSM test shape is released from an F-16D near Edwards AFB. *(Lockheed Martin Corporation)*

The Nose Landing Gear

The nose landing gear assembly is a two-wheel unit that retracts aftward and upward into a relatively large-volume bay directly under the cockpit. After the nose gear has fully retracted, a starboard hinged door closes to port and meets the forward door, which is attached to the nose gear itself. Once the nose landing gear doors are tightly shut, their serrated, or dog-tooth, edges work in concert to help the aircraft's stealth characteristics.

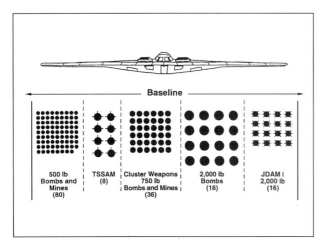

This illustration shows the B-2's baseline conventional-delivery capability with one exception. The eight-TSSAM package, second from left, is now eight JASSM. The TSSAM, formerly known as the AGM-137, was canceled. *(USAF)*

While hitting a speed of Mn 0.92 at an altitude of 200 ft above the Pacific Ocean off Vandenberg AFB, California, B-2 number four (82-1069) dropped a B-83 thermonuclear bomb shape. If needed, a single B-2 could carry 16 B-83s. *(USAF)*

The Main Landing Gear

Each one of the B-2's two main landing gear assemblies has four wheels. When the main landing gear is retracted, each assembly is covered by a single tight-fitting door of large proportion. These "barn" doors close inward toward the aircraft's centerline and feature opposite-angled leading and trailing edges for low-observability characteristics.

Bedding Down the B-2 Fleet

"The components we have seen, the major subassemblies, and the assembled aircraft itself, all attest to a dedicated work force producing a quality product."

—DEFENSE SECRETARY RICHARD B. CHENEY,

JUNE 22, 1989

It was on January 5, 1987—long before anyone out of the know actually knew exactly what the advanced technology bomber even looked like—that United States Congressman Ike Skelton (D. Missouri) made his announcement that Whiteman Air Force Base, Missouri would be the first home of the B-2 Stealth Bomber. Almost six years later, on April 1, 1993, USAF Col. (now Lt. Gen.) Ronald C. Marcotte accepted command of the B-2's operating wing—the 509th Bomb Wing (BW), formerly known as the 509th Bombardment Wing (Heavy). (Col. Marcotte was subsequently promoted to the rank of Brig. Gen. while he was still serving as the 509th BW commander.)

When a newly established USAF wing such as the 509th BW and its operating squadrons start receiving a new type of aircraft for its fleet—especially a special-purpose aircraft like the stealthy B-2—they are tasked with the job of bedding them down. This oftentimes includes the construction of newer and better facilities for the incoming aircraft such as self-contained hangars enjoyed by the B-2s. These individual hangars are purpose-built to meet the maintenance and service demands put forth by these unique aircraft. Moreover, existing base facilities have to be improved to support the new wing's type of aircraft.

Long before the arrival of the first operational B-2A Spirit, this plan for the B-2 fleet bed-down had been put into motion by its original user—the Strategic Air Command (SAC). Then on June 1, 1992, when SAC was

The first arrival of the first fleet aircraft for any USAF wing is a momentous occasion indeed. It was a bit of a dreary day on December 17, 1993, at Whiteman AFB. Nevertheless, the 509th BW's pride and joy overrode the foul weather as its first B-2A made its final approach for landing. *(USAF)*

Touchdown! Drag rudders deployed, landing lights on, and auxiliary engine air inlet doors opened, the eighth B-2A begins to slow down. Exactly 90 years earlier, the Wright Brothers made the first powered and controlled flight of a heavier-than-air vehicle. Their first flight covered a distance of 120 ft, or 52 ft less than the B-2's 172 ft wingspan. *(USAF)*

inactivated, the Air Combat Command (ACC) was simultaneously activated, and it took over the responsibility of correctly fielding the two operating and single training squadrons associated with the fleet of B-2s. The USAF's Air Combat Command is the main provider of combat air forces to the U.S.'s warfighting commands. In addition to vectoring its fleets of B-52H, B-1B, and B-2A bombers, the ACC flies battle-management, electronic-combat, fighter, proficiency trainer, reconnaissance, and rescue aircraft, as well as command, control, communications, and intelligence systems. The ACC is responsible for the 1st Air Force, 8th Air Force, 9th Air Force, and the 12th Air Force. The 509th BW, then, comes under the guidance of the ACC and the legendary 8th Air Force, with its headquarters located at Barksdale AFB, Louisiana.

Whiteman Air Force Base

Whiteman Air Force Base is located in Johnson County, Missouri, 65 miles southeast of Kansas City. The base is 2 miles south of Knob Noster, just off U.S. Highway 50, and is about 10 miles east of Warrensburg and 20 miles west of Sedalia. Whiteman AFB was named for U.S. Army Air Corps Second Lt. George A. Whiteman, the first pilot to die in aerial combat during the Japanese attack on Pearl Harbor. Whiteman AFB has an area of 4,684 acres, an altitude of 869 ft above sea level, and a runway length of 12,400 ft.

The 509th Bomb Wing moved its headquarters from Pease AFB (now Air National Guard Base, ANGB), New Hampshire, to Whiteman AFB in an unmanned and nonoperational status on September 30, 1991. During the next two years, Whiteman's building infrastructure continued to expand as the arrival date of the first B-2 grew closer. The 509th returned to

Its wet runways landing capability already proved, the 509th BW's first operational B-2 (88-0329) sends up a rooster tail as its rolls to a stop at Whiteman. It is interesting to see how such an aerodynamic aircraft deals so well with hydrodynamics. The B-2's lift spoilers and wheel brakes are so efficient, it doesn't require braking parachutes (drag chutes) to aid with its slowing process. *(USAF)*

Commanded by Gen. Mike Loh (left) and piloted by Lt. Col. J. Belanger on its delivery flight from Palmdale, the 509th BW's premier B-2 is home. After it was checked out and found satisfactory, it was placed in one of newly built hangars. The opened auxiliary engine air inlet doors are noteworthy. *(USAF)*

B-2A number eight—later named the Spirit of MISSOURI—is shown here in early 1994 with its two weapons bays' four doors opened and its cockpit entry ladder/door extended. In addition, shown in good detail, the aircraft's four perforated air dams are lowered. These smooth out the high-velocity airstream during weapons release. *(Northrop Grumman)*

As the ninth production B-2A (88-0330), the Spirit of CALIFORNIA taxis out for a training mission takeoff. Its nose landing gear assembly, hawklike nose, and cockpit windows are shown to good advantage. *(Northrop Grumman)*

operational status when personnel from Detachment 509, the base's overseers for the past two years, were formerly assigned to the wing on April 1, 1993. Then on July 1, 1993, the 509th accepted host responsibilities for Whiteman from the Boeing Minuteman II intercontinental ballistic missile (ICBM) operating 351st Missile Wing.

Whiteman's new host unit became the 509th Bomb Wing (BW), which on December 17, 1993, received the first of 21 Northrop Grumman B-2A Spirit bombers. Appropriately, its first B-2 was named the Spirit of MISSOURI.

509th Bomb Wing and Bomb Squadrons

The 509th BW, one of the most famous of all the USAF wings, has historical roots that trace back to its World War II ancestor, the 509th Composite Group (CG). The U.S. Army Air Forces activated the 509th CG on December 17, 1944, at Wendover Army Air Field (AAF), Utah, with only one mission: To drop the atomic bomb. Led by Col. Paul W. Tibbets Jr., the group trained hard for its unique task. In May 1945, the 509th transferred to North Field, Tinian, the Marianas, where the intense training continued. Then on August 6, 1945, the 509th fulfilled its destiny when the Boeing B-29 Superfortress named "Enola Gay," piloted by Col. Tibbets, dropped the first atomic bomb ("Little Boy") and obliterated Hiroshima, Japan. Another B-29 named "Bock's Car" dropped a second atomic bomb ("Fat Man") three days later on August 9 and decimated Nagasaki, Japan. Within days, the Japanese sued for peace and World War II ended.

Upon returning to the United States in late 1945, the first and still only atomic bombardment group settled into Roswell Army Air Field (RAAF), New Mexico. Shortly afterward, it became the core of the newly created Strategic Air Command. In August 1946, the then called 509th Bombardment Group (BG) again traveled to the Pacific, where it participated

The Spirit of KANSAS (89-0127), in the background, and the Spirit of FLORIDA (93-1085) are respectively the twelfth and eighteenth B-2As built. The KANSAS was delivered to the 509th in February 1995, while the FLORIDA was delivered in June 1996. All 21 of the Spirit stealth bomber fleet will be operational sometime in the year 2000. *(USAF)*

As the Spirit of CALIFORNIA's crew chief awaits the aircraft's pilot and mission commander to fly yet another training sortie, circa mid-1995, the rising sun brightly shines through its aft hangar door opening. The aircraft boarding ladder/door is noteworthy. *(Northrop Grumman)*

in Operation Crossroads. During this maneuver, a B-29 named "Dave's Dream" dropped an atomic bomb on an armada of obsolete and captured warships moored off the Bikini Atoll.

On November 17, 1947, SAC activated the 509th Bombardment Wing (BW) at Roswell AAF and assigned the 509th BG to the wing. The significance of the 509th BW emblem's wings represents the branch of service—the USAF—but the wings are not in the familiar outstretched position. When the ancient Greeks approached a stranger, they raised their arms with the palms of their hands outward to show they were carrying no weapons—a sign of peace. The 509th obtained special permission to display the wings in the raised position to show that it, too, comes in peace. The words *Defensor-Vindex* (translation: "Defender-Avenger") means that its mission was, and still is, to protect and retaliate for any infringement on that peace.

The cloud burst represents two things: that the 509th dropped the only two atomic bombs ever in wartime and that it still uses atomic power as a deterrent to war and defender of peace. Finally, the eldest son symbol shows that the wing is the oldest atomic-trained military unit in the world.

On the 90th anniversary of the Wright Brothers' first flight at Kitty Hawk, North Carolina, the first operational B-2A Stealth Bomber was ceremoniously delivered to the 393rd Bomb Squadron (BS)—the Tigers, of the 509th BW at Whiteman AFB. The date was December 17, 1993, and after its flawless delivery flight from Edwards AFB, it touched down just after 2:00 p.m. local time. It was piloted by then ACC Comdr. Gen. John Michael Loh and copiloted by Lt. Col. John Bellanger. The aircraft was the eighth production B-2A (88-0329), or AV-8. The date of its delivery, ironically, also marked the 49th anniversary of the establishment of the

The Spirit of WASHINGTON (88-0332) took center stage in October 1994 at Seattle's Boeing Field during its naming ceremony. As the eleventh production B-2A, the WASHINGTON became the 509th BW's fourth operational Spirit. Boeing, a major supplier of B-2 assemblies—landing gear, outer wings, aft center section, and so on—was more than thrilled to have a B-2 present. *(The Boeing Company)*

This photograph illustrates part of the 509th BW's B-2 hangar facilities and eight of its nine operational (at the time) Spirit bombers parked on the ramp in August 1997. As part of the START (Strategic Arms Reduction Talks) Treaty agreement between Russia and the U.S., the aircraft were parked like this for an open display request from Russia. *(USAF)*

original 509th CG. In a Whiteman AFB ceremony on this very same date, the first operational B-2 was named the Spirit of MISSOURI. The 509th had operated a long series of Boeing aircraft, including the B-29, KB-29M, B-50, B-47, KC-135, B-52 Stratofortress, as well as the General Dynamics FB-111A. Now it was time for the historic 509th BW to gear up for the reception of its new bomber, the Northrop Grumman B-2A Spirit.

In between the first and second B-2A deliveries to the 509th BW, on March 31, 1994, at a ceremony that was held at the B-2's final assembly facility (Site 4) in Palmdale, the USAF bestowed the fleet name of *Spirit* to the B-2 aircraft. The official name is most appropriate, for it embodies the essence of the American dream and the epitome of exactly what Jack Northrop had tried to achieve all along (Table 7-1).

The initial configuration Block 10 B-2As were stealthy, but a basic model. The Block 20s had enhanced avionics and low-observable characteristics. The final Block 30 aircraft have more enhanced avion-

A dramatic head-on view of the 509th BW's first operational B-2A—the Spirit of MISSOURI—as it appeared over Whiteman AFB (lower right) in mid-1995. Appropriately named MISSOURI, since it was the first B-2 in the state, this view highlights the B-2's sinister-looking appearance. *(Northrop Grumman)*

Before his historic return to space as the world's oldest astronaut, U.S. Senator John Glenn (D) of Ohio speaks at the July 18, 1997, ceremony at Wright-Patterson AFB, Ohio to name the fourteenth B-2 (82-1070) the Spirit of OHIO. Each named B-2 has a crest similar to the one shown here on Glenn's podium. *(USAF)*

The Spirit of OHIO was one of the six FSD B-2s (the fifth one) that were thoroughly tested at Edwards AFB and elsewhere. In this scene, the OHIO shows off its "tail" code ED (for Edwards AFB), B-2 Combined Test Force emblem, testing outfit (the 412th Test Group), and Edwards' motto—*AD INEXPLORATA,* Latin for "Toward the Unexplored." *(USAF)*

This late 1998 photograph—just cleared by the USAF, shows the Block 30-status cockpit layout for the Spirit of LOUISIANA (93-1088). Early B-2s were delivered as Block 10 aircraft, then later B-2s as Block 20 aircraft. All Block 10/20 B-2s, after modification, will be Block 30-status aircraft. Compare this B-2 office with the B-2's original cockpit layout in Chapter 6. *(USAF)*

TABLE 7-1 B-2 Delivery Dates to USAF and Arrival Dates at Whiteman AFB

Delivered to USAF	Arrived at Whiteman AFB	AV Number	Name/Date Named
12/11/93	12/17/93	AV-8	MISSOURI; 12/17/93
8/16/94	8/17/94	AV-9	CALIFORNIA; 9/24/94
8/29/94	8/31/94	AV-7	TEXAS; 9/24/94
10/27/94	10/30/94	AV-11	WASHINGTON; 10/29/94
12/29/94	12/30/94	AV-10	SOUTH CAROLINA; 4/15/95
2/16/95	2/17/95	AV-12	KANSAS; 5/13/95
6/26/95	6/28/95	AV-13	NEBRASKA; 9/3/95
9/25/95	11/14/95	AV-14	GEORGIA; 12/11/95
12/21/95	1/10/96	AV-16	HAWAII; 5/27/96
1/12/95	1/24/96	AV-15	ALASKA; 7/27/96
5/13/96	5/15/96	AV-18	OKLAHOMA; 9/14/96
3/29/96	7/3/96	AV-17	FLORIDA; 10/23/96
8/96	8/30/96	AV-19	KITTY HAWK; 12/17/96
10/19/90	7/18/97	AV-2	OHIO; 7/18/97; also known as "The Wright Spirit," "Ship From Hell," and "Murphy's Law"
8/97	8/5/97	AV-20	PENNSYLVANIA; 8/5/97
6/18/91	10/10/97	AV-3	NEW YORK; 10/10/97; also known and "Navigator," "Ghost," and "Afternoon Delight"
11/97	11/10/97	AV-21	LOUISIANA; 11/10/97
10/5/92	3/20/98	AV-5	ARIZONA; 3/20/98; also known as "Fire and Ice," and "Toad"
10/2/92	5/23/98	AV-6	MISSISSIPPI; 5/23/98; known earlier as "Black Widow," "Arnold the Pig," and "Penguin"
2/2/93	1999	AV-4	INDIANA; 5/22/99; known earlier as "Christine"
7/17/89	2000	AV-1	AMERICA (pending); known earlier as "Fatal Beauty"

ics, superior radar modes, far superior terrain following abilities, and increased survivability.

On November 7, 1996, Headquarters ACC activated the 394th Combat Training Squadron (CTS)—the Panthers—at Whiteman AFB, and to train newly appointed B-2 flight crews, it was assigned to the 509th BW. This was the second B-2 flying unit put into operation at Whiteman. The third B-2 flying unit, the 325th BS—once called the Alley Oop—is the second of the two operating B-2 combat units. It was activated on January 8, 1998 (Figs. 7-17, 7-18 and 7-19). Each one of the 509th BW's two operating bomb squadrons, the 325th and 393rd, are responsible for eight B-2As (Fig. 7-20).

The USAF/ACC is constantly searching for highly qualified multiengine pilots to operate its fleet of B-2A Spirit bombers. To accomplish this, in part, it looks for career officers with numerous flying hours at the helm of multiengine bomber aircraft such as the B-52H and B-1B. For example, in June 1998, the USAF selected 19 pilots for B-2 positions within the

The sixth and last FSD B-2 (AV-6, 82-1071) flies near Edwards AFB on June 21, 1994. Upon close examination, it becomes quite apparent that the aircraft's leading edges are not perfectly straight. New-build Block 30 aircraft, as well as the modified Block 10 and 20 aircraft, have stealth-improved leading edges. *(USAF)*

Air Vehicle 1 (82-1066) is shown during its sixth flight and first in-flight refueling test over Rogers Dry Lake and the South Base area at Edwards AFB in late 1989. With a single in-flight fill-up, a B-2's maximum range is extended to more than 10,000 nmi. *(USAF)*

Shown here covered by tarpaulins in March 1994 at USAF Plant 42 in Palmdale are the two B-2 airframes (Northrop build numbers 999 and 1000) that were built to serve as static ground test vehicles. While the one being stored in the background appears to have B-2-styled landing gear, the one in front does not. *(USAF)*

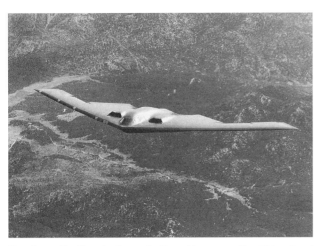

Soaring effortlessly through the skies over the Tehachapi mountains just to the west of Edwards, AV-4 (82-1069) makes yet another successful test flight on November 10, 1993. Its deep, V-shaped belly is noteworthy. *(USAF)*

While flying at an approximate 10° nose-down pitch angle on November 12, 1993, AV-4 tests its fully deployed split drag rudders as speed brakes. When closed, the split drag rudders work as ailerons. *(USAF)*

509th Bomb Wing. Eleven of them, six captains and five majors, entered the B-2 program in the fall of 1998. The other eight, all captains, were selected for the wing's Northrop T-38 Companion Trainer Program (CTP) as instructor pilots and for key staff positions. They began B-2 pilot training in early 1999. The 509th BW has a number of T-38 Talons (reportedly 10 to 12) that it uses for pilot proficiency and training duties.

The 509th had 13 operational B-2As assigned to it at the end of 1996, 17 by the end of 1997, and 19 by the end of 1998. These and some of the later-delivered Block 10 and Block 20 B-2As have been systematically rotated back to Palmdale for their respective Block 30 configuration modification upgrade programs.

With the aforementioned 13 operational B-2As available to the 509th BW on January 1, 1997, except for those in Palmdale, the USAF announced that the fleet had become available for use in a conventional bombardment role as well as nuclear. Thus, on New Year's Day 1997, Headquarters ACC proudly announced an early but limited initial operational capability (IOC) for the Northrop Grumman B-2A Spirit. Initial operational capability for the B-2 approximately coincided with the conclusion of the aircraft's 7-year and 11-month-long flight-test program, which had ended in mid-June 1997. In all, after nearly 1,000 missions, the six FSD B-2s had participated in flight-test, weapons-test, hot weather and cold weather, and numerous other aircraft systems evaluations.

Exactly three months later, on April 1, 1997, Headquarters USAF announced full operational capability (FOC) for the 509th BW's growing fleet of B-2As. The twenty-first and, sadly, the last production B-2A (93-1088) was delivered to the 509th as a Block 30-capable aircraft in November 1997 and as the seventeenth operational stealth bomber.

Flying high above the Mojave Desert, a KC-10A Extender is hooked up and transferring fuel into AV-3 (82-1068) on December 2, 1993. The design contrast between the stealthy B-2 Spirit and the conventional KC-10 aircraft is evident during this aerial refueling mission. *(USAF)*

A B-2 can carry up to 16 2,000 lb class GBU-31 JDAM conventional munitions. Once released, the satellite-guided GBU-31s do not miss their preprogrammed targets. In this view of a B-2 over an Edwards AFB bombing range, two JDAMs head for their respective targets. *(USAF)*

Named the Spirit of WASHINGTON on October 29, 1994, this was the fourth B-2A that was delivered to the 509th BW, 393rd BS. Originally delivered in the Block 10 configuration—stealthy, but a basic model—the WASHINGTON has since been brought up to Block 30 status. *(USAF)*

Shown here during a November 12, 1993, test flight in silhouette, the fourth B-2A Spirit (82-1069) makes its forty-third flight. Known as AV-4, or the fourth of six FSD aircraft, this particular B-2 served as the aerodynamics and performance test bed. *(USAF)*

At this writing, to be delivered in Block 30 configuration remain two more stealth bombers. Respectively, these two remaining B-2As, to be the twentieth and twenty-first operational aircraft, AV-4 (82-1069) and AV-1 (81-1066), are undergoing Block 30 modifications in Palmdale. The former was scheduled for delivery in late spring or early summer 1999, while the latter is scheduled for delivery in June 2000. Neither aircraft has been named at this writing, but according to a Northrop Grumman spokesperson, the last one to be delivered might be named the Spirit of AMERICA; ironically, it was the very first B-2 built.

On June 11, 1995, the Spirit of MISSOURI visited the Paris Air Show. Flown from the U.S. by then 509th BW commander Brig. Gen. Ronald Marcotte and acting mission commander Maj. Jim Smith, the aircraft appeared for 1 hr and 20 min before departing. It is shown touching down at Le Bourget field. (Northrop Grumman)

The B-2 Combined Test Force (CTF)—consisting of Northrop Grumman, Boeing, General Electric, and the USAF—which numbered about 2,000 people at its peak, exhaustively tested all aspects of the B-2 Spirit. Some of the many aircraft capabilities evaluated by the B-2 CTF included low observability, or stealth, low-altitude terrain avoidance/terrain following, radar, navigation, flight controls, flying qualities, loads, structures, weapons delivery, and both cold and warm climate functionality. The B-2 CTF logged nearly 5,000 flight-test hours in some 1,000 flights (an average of 5 hours per flight) and accomplished 23,500 flight-test points. All of the B-2s used in flight-test have been or will be upgraded to Block 30 standard and delivered to the USAF and its 509th BW. As of August 1, 1999, five of them have joined the 509th BW. The sixth and last FSD B-2A is to join the 509th BW in mid-2000.

The B-2 in Service

The USAF—in particular, its Air Combat Command—has taken delivery of its B-2s in three configuration blocks: Blocks 10, 20, and 30. Initial delivery was 6 FSD aircraft, 10 aircraft in the Block 10 configuration, 3 in the Block 20 configuration, and 2 in the Block 30 configuration.

Block 10-configured B-2s provide limited combat capability with no capability to launch conventional guided weapons such as the AGM-154 JSOW. The Block 10 model carries only Mk 84 2,000-lb class conventional bombs or gravity nuclear weapons. The B-2s in this configuration are used primarily for training.

Block 20-configured Spirits have an interim capability to launch nuclear and conventional munitions, including some of the GPS-guided (Global Positioning System) munitions. The Block 20 has been tested with the Mk 84 and the CBU-87/-87B Combined Effects Munition (CEM) cluster bombs at low altitude during full-bay releases.

Block 30-configured aircraft are fully capable and meet the essential employment capabilities defined by the USAF. The first fully configured Block 30 aircraft, the Spirit of PENNSYLVANIA (AV-20, 93-1087), was delivered to the 509th BW on August 7, 1997. These aircraft have the ability to deliver all versions of the JDAM munitions, the JSOW, and other satellite-guided weapons.

All Block 10, 20, and the six FSD aircraft are to eventually be brought up to Block 30 standard. The Block 30 configuration modification processes began at Northrop Grumman's Palmdale Site 4 facility in July 1995 and are scheduled for completion in June 2000. It remains to be seen if additional block configuration programs will be warranted.

At an estimated cost of $2.1 billion a copy, the United States was only able to fund a small number of Northrop Grumman B-2A Spirit aircraft. The original plan in the mid-1980s was

Each one of the 509th BW's B-2 aircraft lives within its own special hangar. After their respective missions are over, they are gone over thoroughly by their highly trained maintenance crews. Before long, they are once again mission-capable. *(USAF)*

to procure 132 operational B-2s. This was subsequently reduced to 75, then 20. (The number went up to 21 when the first B-2 was added to the operational fleet.)

Looking ahead toward the twenty-first century and beyond, with only these 21 B-2A Spirit stealth bomber aircraft available for use, a serious question remains to be answered: Are there enough B-2s available to protect the U.S. and its worldwide interests? At this writing, the USAF Air Combat Command is structured for a total inventory of 187 heavy bombardment aircraft, including 83 B-52Hs, 83 B-1Bs, and 21 B-2As. Also as of this writing, the youngest operational B-52H is nearly 38 years old. The B-52Hs have survived only because of their numerous and expensive modification programs—including the rewinging of all B-52Hs. Although the fleet of B-1B Lancers is relatively new—the youngest operational B-1B is presently more than 11 years old—they will not be able to soldier on without expensive modification programs like those accorded the B-52.

Normal wear and tear and accidental attrition will be the worst enemy of the B-2. Although highly skilled USAF maintenance personnel will do their very best to keep them flying, no mechanically driven being can last forever without expensive modification programs. These would probably be conducted at the Oklahoma City Air Logistics Center at Tinker AFB, Oklahoma.

The B-2 in Combat

"If I had to guess, based on historical perspectives, we measure miss distances with a yard stick."

—BRIG. GEN. LEROY BARDNIDGE JR., MARCH 25, 1999

On March 24, 1999, less than two years after it had achieved Initial Operational Capability (IOC) with the 509th Bomb Wing, the Northrop Grumman B-2A Spirit began to earn its spurs as a full-fledged combat aircraft in its operational debut, participating in the first manned combat missions of Operation Noble Anvil. During the first mission of the operation, two unidentified crews and two B-2As, each loaded with 16 GBU-31 2,000-lb class JDAM weapons, took off in the early morning hours of March 24 and flew nonstop to drop their 32 JDAMs on targets in the former Republic of Yugoslavia. The aircraft flew the 31-hr mission nonstop from Whiteman to the target area and back, landing on the morning of March 25. The stealth bombers followed air- and sea-launched cruise missile attacks and were the first manned aircraft over the targets. (The GBU-31 JDAM is derived from either the Mk-84 or BLU-109 unguided munitions.)

After takeoff, the first two B-2s of the operation flew about 13 hours with several midair refuelings, spent about 5 hours loitering nearby, and then attacked multiple targets. Then they flew another 13 hours or so back to Whiteman.

Operation Noble Anvil was initiated to support NATO's Operation Allied Force against Serbian aggression. According to President Bill Clinton in a televised announcement of March 24, the campaign has three objectives:

1. To demonstrate the seriousness of NATO's opposition to aggression and its support of peace.

2. To deter Yugoslav President Slobodan Milosevic from escalating his attacks on civilians by imposing a price for those attacks.

3. To seriously diminish Serbia's military capabilities and abilities to wage war against Kosovo in the future.

Brig. Gen. Leroy Barnidge Jr., commander of the 509th BW, said, "The jets performed perfectly and the crews performed even better," while addressing the media on the flight line after the first two B-2s had returned safely to Whiteman on March 25. He said the B-2 is different from other bombers in the inventory [B-52Hs and B-1Bs] because of "its ability to be able to manage the energy that is put into the air by radar sites around the world. This jet is very, very good at what it's designed to do."

"This airplane does everything it's advertised to do and more, but it's only a piece of hardware," Barnidge said. "It's the people who make it happen, from those who designed and built it, to those who operate and maintain it every day—they make it as good as it is." Referring to the value of stealth, Barnidge said the B-2 "saves lives by putting fewer Americans in harm's way while going after critical heavily defended targets."

The 509th BW's two operational bomb squadrons—the 325th BS and 393rd BS—were in the operation from day one. Col. Tony Imondi, 509th Operations Group commander, said on March 25, "The crews chosen to fly these missions are the most experienced in the wing." Imondi selected the crews based on their experience in combat and B-2 operations. "The B-2 was designed to deliver weapons on the first day—yesterday was the first day of the war and the B-2 was there," Imondi added.

Congressman Ike Skelton, a leading supporter of the B-2 program since its inception, said, "I'm immensely proud of the B-2 pilots and all the personnel at Whiteman Air Force Base. I know that all Missourians and all Americans will welcome them home from their difficult and dangerous mission."

Lt. Gen. Ron Marcotte, 8th Air Force commander in charge of the B-2 fleet, a B-2 pilot himself and the first commander of the 509th BW, said, "It was particularly heartening to see the B-2 kind of graduate and demonstrate its tremendous capability."

"The air defense system in Yugoslavia is very capable, and it poses considerable threat," said Army Gen. Henry Shelton, chairman of the Joint Chiefs of Staff. This was realized a few days into the war when, for the first time, a stealth aircraft was lost in combat.

Although the exact reason for its loss is unclear at this writing, a Lockheed Martin F-117A Nighthawk of the 8th Fighter Squadron, 49th Fighter Wing based at Holloman AFB in New Mexico, went down in Yugoslavia on March 27 some 30 miles west of Belgrade. The pilot ejected safely and was rescued about 6 hr after the crash. Whether it was shot down by a SA-3 surface-to-air missile (SAM) as first rumored or was lost due to a mechanical failure or pilot error remains to be seen. By April 11, though not yet officially announced, speculation had it that the F-117A was downed by "a lucky shot." (The F-117A that was lost was named *Something Wicked* in Operation Desert Storm, carried tail number 82-0806, and was the twenty-first of 59 delivered aircraft.)

The B-2s are not invulnerable either, and a loss of one or more would create major adversity for the USAF. A reduction in the already-sparse fleet of only 21 B-2s (20 in service by mid-1999, with no more new ones being built) would be an unacceptable situation for the U.S. Armed Forces, and a bitter blow to the United States' stealth aircraft program on the whole.

On March 29, 1999, Col. Bill Hood, 509th Logistics Group commander, said the aircraft "are performing better than expected." "We have met every tasking and are sustaining our combat performance," he added.

Each time a jet lands, maintainers prepare it for the next scheduled combat mission. "We are prepared to sustain combat operations indefinitely," Hood said. The skin of the plane—made of composite materials designed to absorb and deflect radar—is "holding up very well," Hood added. "This should lay to rest concerns people may have about the aircraft's stealthiness." Col. Hood ended with "The planes are performing very, very well. We are quite pleased," adding that the "plane is allowing crews to put bombs on target as advertised."

Capt. Matt Kmon, 393rd BS B-2 maintenance officer, said maintainers used standard recovery operations for the first four jets taking part in the combat missions. "Obviously, during a 30-hr flight we'd expect more than just minor maintenance," said Kmon. Comparing the mission to a long drive in a car, he said that after a 30-hr car trip, "you might have to add some oil."

While jets returned home needing some minor repairs, the B-2s received no combat scrapes. "They look great," Kmon said. "They're landing [in] better [shape] than on day-to-day training sorties."

"The relatively new GBU-31 JDAM weapons are also doing good work," according to a Defense Department official. The official said the B-2 was selected because of its heavy payload—by comparison, the F-117 stealth fighter attack aircraft can only carry two 2,000-lb. bombs. The B-2's ability to attack multiple targets, and its ability to drop weapons precisely at night and in all weather conditions, was the deciding factor. The satellite-guidance system on the B-2's conventional bombs can direct the explosive to a programmed target without any visible contact or laser-designator as used by the F-117.

Also on March 29, 1999, five B-1Bs were deployed to Europe in support of NATO operations, marking a milestone in modern bomber aircraft history. Operation Allied Force is the first time the USAF's heavy bombardment aircraft fleet—comprised of the Boeing B-52H Stratofortress, Boeing North American B-1B Lancer, and Northrop Grumman B-2A Spirit—"are [being] used together operationally," according to Maj. J.C. Valle, deputy chief of ACC's Weapons and Tactics Branch. (The B-1B made its combat debut on December 1, 1998, in the skies over Iraq during Operation Desert Fox.)

"The B-2's low-observable, or 'stealth,' characteristics give it the unique ability to penetrate an enemy's most sophisticated defenses and threaten its most valued, and heavily defended, targets. During the operation the B-2 is being used in a direct attack role employing Global Positioning System-guided munitions," said Valle.

"This major milestone for the bomber force shows the pride and professionalism of the entire Air Combat Command team," said Lt. Gen. Tom Keck, ACC vice commander. "We're also proving that the Air Force is ready and continues to employ the Expeditionary Aerospace Force (AEF) concept."

Capt. Kmon said, "We've met every tasking and we are very confident that we can meet any future taskings. If the war-fighting commander calls for one [B-2], we give him one—if he calls for two, we give him two. All the maintainers are putting forth their best and it shows."

On April 5, 1999 Brig. Gen. Barnidge said, "The world called and we responded." He added, "Everyone associated with Whiteman and the B-2 has as much to be proud of as the crews who actually put the bombs on target—it's an absolute world-class team effort."

Dateline: June 11, 1999. The Day the Bombing Stopped

America's strategic bomber force proved itself worthy during Operation Allied Force.

Working in concert during the operation, the B-52H had, as of this writing, been used as a standoff air-launched cruise missile platform bomber, firing its weapons from outside Serbian territory. The B-1B was being used as both a guided and unguided weapons delivery system. The B-2, throughout the operation, launched satellite-guided 2000-lb class GBU-31 JDAM munitions with near pinpoint accuracy.

As of this writing, NATO's Operation Allied Force had just ended after 79 days of continuous bombardment. As far as the B-2A Spirit was concerned, according to 509th BW Public Affairs chief Capt. William "Brett" Ashworth in an e-mail to this writer dated June 28, 1999, "Our final numbers were: More than 45 missions flown. Dropped more than 1.3 million pounds of ordnance. Flew less than 1% of sorties, but dropped 11% of bombs. We did not fly two aircraft each time. There were times when we flew a single aircraft. And all aircraft flown were Block 30s. At this time we aren't releasing the names of aircrews who flew missions."

The B-2 of 2002

"I justify it [the B-2] because I think the prime responsibility of a president is the national security of the
United States, and I'm determined to put forth a program that is sound in every way."

— PRESIDENT GEORGE BUSH, JULY 24, 1989

When the year 2002 arrives, about three years from this writing, the 509th Bomb Wing
and its two combat Bomb Squadrons (the 325th and 393rd) will be operating all 21
B-2A aircraft. Initial operational capability (IOC) with the 393rd BS—the first of the
509th's two combat squadrons—was achieved on April 1, 1997. Full operational capability
(FOC) with the 325th BS—the second combat squadron—is to be met in mid-2000.

At this writing, in three blocks of capability, the B-2s are capable of the following missions: (1) Block 10 aircraft (aircraft numbers 2 through 16 can carry B61 or B83 nuclear
bombs or 16 Mk 84 2,000-lb class conventional bombs; (2) Block 20 aircraft (numbers 17
through 19) will also carry the B61 or B83 nuclear bombs, and GPS-Aided Targeting Sys-
tem/GPS-Aided Munition (GATS/GAM), to permit an "early, interim, near-precision" strike
capability; and (3) the only production Block 30 aircraft (numbers 20 and 21) feature full

Dwarfed by a McDonnell Douglas (now Boeing) KC-10A Extender, a B-2 receives an in-flight drink of
jet petroleum fuel. Reportedly, whether by KC-135s or KC-10s, all in-flight refueling tests were successful. In fact, B-2 test pilots reported that there were no problems whatsoever. *(USAF)*

If a low-observable (stealth) aircraft is to be "invisible" to enemy radar, it must have a very, very low RCS at its front. While having a very low RCS from its top, bottom, sides, and rear is critical to its survival, it is the aircraft's front that an enemy radar would see first. *(Northrop Grumman)*

While the B-2 is fully optimized for high-altitude bombardment missions, a major part of its Single Integrated Operational Plan (SIOP) incorporates low-level bombardment. It has been realized for a number of years now that it is easier to penetrate enemy airspace at high subsonic speed and at "treetop" level. *(Northrop Grumman)*

precision-guided munitions (PGM) capability, including up to sixteen 2,000-lb class JDAMs on the rotary launcher assemblies, and will carry up to 80 Mk 82 500-lb class conventional bombs, cluster munitions, including sensor-fused weapons (SFW), the Mk 117 750-lb class conventional bomb, and the Mk 36 and Mk 62 aerial mines on bomb rack assemblies (BRA).

Other Block 30 enhancements include fully operational defensive and offensive avionics, a more sophisticated mission planning system, and additional operating modes for the aircraft's two Hughes AN/APQ-181 low probability of intercept (LPI) synthetic aperture radar (SAR) system. Additionally, Block 30s incorporate configuration changes required to make B-2s conform to the defined RCS: replacement of the aft decks, installation of remaining defensive avionics suites, and installation of a contrail (engine exhaust trail) management system.

The B-2A's wholly unique "double W"-shaped trailing edges have many movable surfaces. These include split drag rudder/speed brake with aileron function, outboard and inboard elevons, and a gust load alleviation system flap. Moreover, to help elude its detection by radar, the trailing edges are saw-toothed. *(Northrop Grumman)*

B-2 Myths and Realities

It has been rumored that the B-2 cannot fly its missions in the rain because its stealth coatings will come off. According to the USAF, rain is not a deterrent to a B-2 mission once the aircraft has been properly prepared and launched. On real combat missions, B-2 crew members would prefer rain because it would hurt the performance of enemy air defense systems.

It has also been said that it is so hard to maintain the B-2's stealth features that the aircraft are hardly ever ready for action. The USAF replies that the B-2 features a high mission capability rate for such a recently fielded aircraft. It adds that it has a higher availability rate than many earlier aircraft had at a comparable

This extreme close-up view of B-2A number one (82-1066), circa 1989, illustrates in great detail the aircraft's three emergency escape hatch locations, opened in-flight refueling receptacle, and heavily sculptured engine air inlets and exhaust cooling scoops just beneath. *(USAF)*

In making the B-2 work, Northrop's Irv Waaland and John Cashen did their respective jobs very well indeed. For just like a camera's view—looking different every time and from every angle—the Spirit looks just as different to radar. *(USAF)*

time, and its availability rate will rise rapidly as the early model Block 10 and Block 20 aircraft—delivered to facilitate training and early operations—are put into final Block 30 configuration.

Also reported is that B-2s have to be protected within special environmental shelters (hangars), or they will be badly damaged. The USAF response is that the B-2 is designed and built to fly in the rain and to stand alert, outdoors, in severe weather. Nearly two weeks of continuous exposure during an Alaskan winter and months of all-weather testing in a USAF climatic chamber have proven the B-2's resistance to the elements.

Skeptics also say that exotic hangars are required to make repairs on the B-2. The USAF response is that some work does require application of paint, tape, and/or caulking materials. As is the case with nonstealthy aircraft maintenance, such materials will not adhere properly if work is done in rain or under other extreme conditions. But just as with other aircraft, most B-2 maintenance can be done without shelters.

Other disbelievers claim that the B-2 cannot be deployed overseas because foreign bases do not have the required shelters. To this the USAF replied that most airports around the

With its landing gear down and locked, landing lights on, split drag rudder/speed brake deployed, and its four auxiliary engine air doors opened, the soon to be named Spirit of WASHINGTON prepared to land at Boeing Field in Seattle, Washington, on October 28, 1994. *(The Boeing Company)*

Not visible from the ground, this B-2 appears to be floating over a thick layer of clouds. One of the B-2's primary infrared signature (heat) reduction devices is, of course, its engine exhaust nozzles and outlets. Incorporated into the top of the wing, the aircraft's pair of engine exhaust "trenches" are optimized to work in unison with the airflow and exhaust flow to minimize the B-2's IR signature. *(USAF)*

The B-2's four nonafterburning General Electric F118 turbofan engines combine to give the aircraft a maximum sea level static thrust rating of 69,200 lb. Other sources have reported a maximum of 76,000 lb, but according to the official USAF fact sheet on the B-2 Spirit, it is 69,200 lb. The Spirit of NEBRASKA (89-0128) is shown. *(Northrop Grumman)*

After its December 17, 1993, landing at Whiteman AFB, the first operational B-2A Spirit (88-0329) taxis behind a follow-me vehicle (not shown) to its designated parking area. The 509th BW has received another 18 B-2 aircraft since this one arrived, with two more to come—one in 1999 and the other in 2000. *(USAF)*

With mission commander Gen. Mike Loh (then ACC commander) and pilot Lt. Col. J. Belanger still in the cockpit, the first operational B-2's ground crew begins to prepare the aircraft for its stay at Whiteman AFB. The opened weapons bays and extended spoiler panels are noteworthy. *(USAF)*

An unknown B-2 ventures fearlessly over a radar test range in 1994 to demonstrate its survivability. These tests were completely successful, and the B-2 proved to be even more survivable than the highly elusive F-117 stealth fighter. For one example, when the soon to be named Spirit of WASHINGTON flew into Seattle's Boeing Field, one of the local TV stations put a Washington Highway Patrol radar gun on it, and the large aircraft did not register. *(USAF)*

Just a great in-flight study of the sixth FSD B-2 (82-1071) during a test hop on July 14, 1994. Nicknamed "Black Widow," the aircraft was so trouble-free its respective ground crews at Edwards AFB called it "The Easy Maintenance." As the nineteenth operational B-2A, it is now the Spirit of MISSISSIPPI. (USAF)

The B-2's two weapons bays have two very large doors made of composite materials. Here, FSD B-2 number four, the performance and weapons development aircraft, tests the aircraft's aerodynamics with all four of its bomb bay doors opened. This particular aircraft, delivered as the twentieth operational B-2 in 1999, was nicknamed "Deadly Attraction" and then "Christine" during its test days at Edwards. (USAF)

world capable of sustaining commercial airliners would have one or more shelters adequate for supporting B-2 operations. The USAF concluded that it is conducting a study of existing facilities worldwide to identify potential B-2 forward-basing options and sheltering concepts.

Beyond the B-2

No one knows if the B-2 will be the last manned bomber or not. There are many possibilities, including the development of an Unmanned Bombardment Air Vehicle (UBAV) similar in concept to the current studies on the Unmanned Combat Air Vehicle. However, given

As it soars some 20,000 ft above ground level on an early test flight, the premier B-2 comes up for a rendezvous with a tanker in late 1989. Nicknamed "Fatal Beauty" during tests, it is to be the twenty-first and last B-2 delivered to the 509th BW. Its operational name, the Spirit of AMERICA, is pending. (USAF)

Named the Spirit of GEORGIA on December 11, 1995, the eighth operational B-2A (89-0129) is all snuggled up within its hangar at Whiteman AFB. The aircraft's opened crew-entry door and ladder is noteworthy. (USAF)

The Spirit of OKLAHOMA (93-1085), the first Block 20 B-2A delivered and now the last one to be upgraded to Block 30 status, left Whiteman AFB in January 1999 for the Northrop Grumman modification line in Palmdale. The Block 30 modification brings more advanced avionics, almost double the radar modes, far superior terrain-following abilities, and increased survivability. *(USAF)*

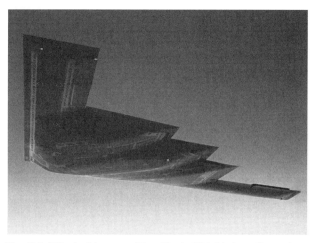

The B-2 "Blocks" began with a Block 10 initial configuration. The Block 20s had enhanced avionics and low-observable characteristics, which not only increased their combat effectiveness, but also their survivability. On October 8, 1996, three Block 20s went against 16 targets at the Nellis AFB, Nevada range complex. Sixteen JDAM weapons were dropped; 16 targets were killed. *(USAF)*

the tremendous cost of the B-2 program and the decline in the defense budget, a successor is many years in the future.

Whatever happens to the B-2 during its tenure with the USAF is not predictable. Yet if the history of bombers from the past is any indication—especially a bomber like the venerable B-52—the B-2 should be around for many, many years.

According to Capt. David Miller, 325th BS maintenance officer, the 509th BW will see increased combat capability, because Block 30s incorporate a dramatically improved self-diagnostic system. "Our flying mission lives and dies by our ability to quickly and accurately troubleshoot faults," said Capt. Miller. Now a Block 30 and named the Spirit of MISSISSIPPI, this shows AV-6 during a test hop on July 14, 1994. *(USAF)*

The Block 30s use a thin-tape process that replaces caulking used on Block 20s. "The thin tape is much more durable than the caulk and drastically reduces the labor requirement after flights," said Maj. Michael Andress, 509th BW Maintenance Squadron maintenance supervisor. Additionally, Maj. Andress said that the number of low observable write-ups have been slashed by a factor of five when comparing Block 30s to the Block 20s. *(USAF)*

B-2 Specifications

Mission	Heavy class multirole strategic bomber capable of delivering conventional, nuclear, and standoff munitions
User	USAF Air Combat Command, 8th Air Force, 509th Bomb Wing (BW); 325th and 393rd Bomb Squadrons (BS), and 394th Combat Training Squadron (CTS); Whiteman AFB, MO; Tail Code WM; Wing motto: Invisible Defenders
Crew	Two; pilot/mission commander, copilot/systems operator, with provision for a third crew member if future missions require it
Power plant	Four nonafterburning General Electric turbofan engines; F118-GE-100 17,300-lb (7,847-kg) thrust class
Fuel capacity	25,385 gals
Height	17.0 ft, 0 in (5.1 m)
Length	69.0 ft, 0 in (20.9 m)
Wingspan	172 ft, 0 in (52.12 m)
Wing area	5,140 sq ft (477,051 sq m)
Empty weight	125,000 lbs (56,700 kg)
Takeoff weight (typical)	336,500 lb (152,635 kg)
Weapons payload	40,000 lb (18,144 kg)
Maximum speed at sea level	Mn 0.95 (525 kt or 972 kmph)
Maximum speed at altitude	High subsonic (Mn 0.95)
Maximum range	6,305 nmi (11,675 km) without aerial refueling; 10,000-plus nmi with one aerial refueling
Service ceiling	50,000 ft (15,152 m)
Armament	Conventional, nuclear, and precision weapons

Conventional	Nuclear	Precision
80 Mk 36 Mine		
36 Mk 62 Mine		
80 Mk 82	16 B61	8 GBU-27
16 Mk 84	16 B83	12 2,000-pound class GBU-31 JDAM
36 CBU-87	16 AGM-129	8 AGM-154 JSOW
36 CBU-89	16 AGM-131	8 AGM-158 JASSAM
36 CBU-97		8 GAM-113

B-2 Production

Air Vehicle Number	Northrop Grumman Build & USAF Serial Numbers
AV-0	999; no USAF serial number; empty airframe; static test article; purposely destroyed
AV-00	1000; no USAF serial number; empty airframe; airframe durability test article
AV-1	1001; 82-1066
AV-2	1002; 82-1067
AV-3	1003; 82-1068
AV-4	1004; 82-1069
AV-5	1005; 82-1070
AV-6	1006; 82-1071
AV-7	1007; 88-0328
AV-8	1008; 88-0329
AV-9	1009; 88-0330
AV-10	1010; 88-0331
AV-11	1011; 88-0332
AV-12	1012; 89-0127
AV-13	1013; 89-0128
AV-14	1014; 89-0129
AV-15	1015; 90-0040
AV-16	1016; 90-0041
AV-17	1017; 92-0700
AV-18	1018; 93-1085
AV-19	1019; 93-1086
AV-20	1020; 93-1087
AV-21	1021; 93-1088

B-2 Aircraft Names

A/C S/N	A/C Name	Date Named
82-1066	Spirit of AMERICA (suggested and pending)	??-??-00
82-1067	Spirit of ARIZONA	03-20-98
82-1068	Spirit of NEW YORK	10-10-97
82-1069	Spirit of INDIANA	05-22-99
82-1070	Spirit of OHIO	07-15-97
82-1071	Spirit of MISSISSIPPI	05-23-98
88-0328	Spirit of TEXAS	09-24-94
88-0329	Spirit of MISSOURI	12-17-93
88-0330	Spirit of CALIFORNIA	03-31-94
88-0331	Spirit of SOUTH CAROLINA	04-15-95
88-0332	Spirit of WASHINGTON	10-29-94
89-0127	Spirit of KANSAS	05-15-95
89-0128	Spirit of NEBRASKA	09-03-95
89-0129	Spirit of GEORGIA	12-11-95
90-0040	Spirit of ALASKA	07-27-96
90-0041	Spirit of HAWAII	05-27-96
92-0700	Spirit of FLORIDA	10-25-96
93-1085	Spirit of OKLAHOMA	09-14-96
93-1086	Spirit of KITTY HAWK	12-17-96
93-1087	Spirit of PENNSYLVANIA	08-05-97
93-1088	Spirit of LOUISIANA	11-10-97

Block 10/20/30 B-2 Delivery Dates*

AF Serial Number	Date of Delivery as Block 10/20/30
82-1066	June 2000 (projected) as Block 30
82-1067	03-20-98 as Block 30
82-1068	10-10-97 as Block 30
82-1069	June 1999 (projected) as Block 30
82-1070	07-18-97 as Block 20
82-1071	05-23-98 as Block 30
88-0328	08-31-94 as Block 10; returned to Palmdale 11-09-95 to undergo upgrading to Block 30 status
88-0329	12/17/93 as Block 10
88-0330	08-17-94 as Block 10
88-0331	12-30-94 as Block 10
88-0332	10-29-94 as Block 10
89-0127	02-17-95 as Block 10
89-0128	06-28-95 as Block 10
89-0129	11-14-95 as Block 10
90-0040	01-24-96 as Block 10
90-0041	01-10-96 as Block 10
92-0700	07-03-96 as second Block 20
93-1085	05-15-96 as first Block 20
93-1086	08-30-96 as Block 20
93-1087	08-05-97 as first Block 30
93-1088	11-10-97 as second Block 30

*Author's note: At this writing, Block 30 B-2As are to be the most capable of the brood.

Block 30 B-2 Delivery Dates (Final Block, at This Writing)

Date of Delivery	USAF Serial Number	A/C Name
08/05/97	93-1087	Spirit of PENNSYLVANIA
10/10/97	82-1068	Spirit of NEW YORK
11/10/97	93-1088	Spirit of LOUISIANA
03/20/98	82-1067	Spirit of ARIZONA

B-2 Chronology

1946

June 25   The world's first flying wing bomber, the piston-powered Northrop XB-35, made a successful first flight from Hawthorne, California, to Edwards AFB (then Muroc AAF) about 100 mi northeast. The second of two XB-35s made its first flight on June 26, 1947.

1947

October 21   The first of two jet-powered flying wing bombers, the Northrop YB-49, made its first flight. These were created from two piston-powered YB-35s.

1948

January 13   The second eight-jet YB-49 made its first flight.

May 15   The first service test Northrop YB-35 flying wing bomber aircraft made its first flight.

June 5   The second YB-49 crashed mysteriously, and its crew was lost. One of its crew, USAF Capt. Glen W. Edwards, was forever immortalized when the USAF later renamed Muroc AAF as Edwards AFB.

1950

May 4   The last example of a flying wing bomber, the six-jet Northrop YRB-49A, made its first flight. It, like the two YB-49s, was created from one of the original XB/YB-35 airframes. The one-of-a-kind YRB-49A was withdrawn from flight status in 1951, and with its retirement, Jack Northrop's dream of producing a fleet of flying wing bombers for the USAF had ended.

1980

August 22 Secretary of Defense Harold Brown officially disclosed the existence of "a number" of stealth aircraft programs, including the Advanced Technology Bomber (ATB) program.

1981

February 18 Mr. John K. Northrop, founder of Northrop Aircraft Corporation and the U.S.'s strongest advocate of flying wing aircraft, passed away after a long illness.

October 20 It was announced that the Northrop/Boeing team had won the ATB competition with the Northrop model N-14 *Senior Ice* entry. At the time, IOC was to occur in mid- to late 1987; also, at the time, 132 advanced technology bombers (ATBs) were to be procured.

1982

Mid-1982 Northrop test pilot Dick Thomas successfully completed the first of 135 flight tests (about 250 total flying hours) of the Northrop-built Tacit Blue aircraft; the flight test program ended in 1985. Code-named the Tacit Blue (Whale), the twin-tailed, platypus-billed aircraft was powered by two nonafterburning Garrett ATF3-6 turbofan engines, like those employed by the Falcon 20 aircraft. The Tacit Blue (Whale) was extensively tested by Northrop and the USAF's 6513th Test Squadron to further investigate low observability of aircraft for the upcoming Northrop ATB, YF-23A, and others. Its radar cross section was "below that of a bat, somewhere down in that area," according to Lt. Gen. George K. Muellner, at its public unveiling in mid-1996. This one-of-a-kind stealth test bed now resides at the U.S. Air Force Museum in Dayton, Ohio.

1985

February 9 A Pentagon budget document revealed an USAF proposal for a $2.3 billion project named *Aurora*. In the budget document, the USAF was asking for $80.1 million for Aurora for fiscal year 1986 and its request increased to $2.3 billion for FY87. The so-called Aurora, thought to be a secret code name for a very advanced type of hypersonic aircraft, turned out to be the code name for the ATB competition funding.

August 10 The ATB has the shape of a flying wing, essentially an aircraft with no fuselage or tail. Senator Barry Goldwater (R-Ariz.), chairman of the Senate Armed Services Committee, said through an aid, "It does look like a flying wing."

1987

January 5 Missouri Congressman Ike Skelton announced that Whiteman AFB, Missouri, had been selected as the home base of the B-2.

November 19 The sum of $2 billion was appropriated for the initial production of four B-2As.

1988

April 21 The USAF ended eight years of secrecy about its ATB as it released a single photograph—an artist concept—of the tailless all-flying wing aircraft.

November 10   Having been rumored to exist for several years, the actual existence of a stealth fighter—the Lockheed F-117A—was officially announced as a real entity during a press conference held at the Pentagon.

November 22   The premier B-2 (82-1066)—Air Vehicle 1, or AV-1—made its official public debut during its rollout ceremonies at Northrop's Palmdale, California, Site 4 facility at U.S. Air Force Plant 42.

November 30   In response to an official request from Wing Commander Col. Orin L. Godsey to preserve the 509th's bombardment aircraft heritage, SAC announced that the 509th Ballistic Missile Wing (BMW) would transfer to Whiteman AFB to become the first B-2 Bomb Wing (BW).

1989

May 11   The first "confirmed" ground run of B-2 number one's four F118-GE-100 turbofan engines occurred at Northrop's Site 4 facility at Palmdale.

July 10   B-2 number one began a scheduled series of low-, medium-, and high-speed taxi test runs at Palmdale to check its steering, braking, and so on in preparation for its maiden flight. It reached a maximum speed of 90 kt on the final run.

July 17   B-2 number one (AV-1) successfully completed a 2-hr and 12-min first flight from Palmdale to the Air Force Flight Test Center at Edwards AFB; it departed Palmdale at 6:38 a.m. local time.

August 16   The second flight of AV-1 was completed. The flight was cut short after the aircraft developed what USAF officials termed a "minor problem" with its auxiliary power system. It flew about one hour of its scheduled 3- to 4-hr mission.

August 26   B-2 number one made its third test flight; 4 hr, 36 min.

September 21   The first B-2 made its fourth flight; 2 hr, 53 min.

November 8   Featuring its first aerial refueling during a 6-hr, 5-min flight, B-2 number one completed its sixth flight. Several hookups and disconnects were performed prior to taking on more than 40,000 lb of JP-8 fuel.

November 18   Air Vehicle 1 made its seventh flight; 7 hr, 17 min.

November 22   One year after its rollout, B-2 number one completed its eighth flight; 5 hr, 48 min. It then entered a scheduled layup.

1990

April 27   The first B-2 completed its ninth flight: 6 hr, 5 min.

May 3   For the first time, the first B-2 was flown with an all-USAF crew. The flight lasted 7 hr, 23 min and was flown by Lt. Cols. Tom LeBeau and John Small. It was the aircraft's tenth flight.

May 11   B-2 number one completed its eleventh flight.

May 22   Just four days after its twelfth flight, AV-1 completed its thirteenth flight.

June 2   B-2 number one completed its fifteenth flight. At this time the aircraft had 64.9 hr of flight time.

June 13   The first B-2 entered its second scheduled layup, after completing its sixteenth flight.

June 30   The premier B-2, as certified by the U.S. General Accounting Office, completed Block 1 testing, verifying its basic flight worthiness.

July 1   Headquarters SAC at Offutt AFB, Nebraska, activated Detachment 509, 100th Air Division, at Whiteman AFB and assigned Col. John J. Donnelly as commander. The personnel of the detachment would oversee B-2 bed-down operations and form the nucleus for the 509th BMW when it became operational at Whiteman AFB.

July 27   It was announced that B-2 number two had entered into the final stages of its manufacturing processes after leaving its final assembly area.

September   The Air Force Association (AFA) awarded the B-2 test team its prestigious Theodore von Karman Award for the most outstanding contribution in the field of science and engineering.

September 30   Effective 12:01 a.m., Headquarters 509th BMW transferred from Pease AFB, New Hampshire, to Whiteman AFB, Missouri, without personnel or equipment, where it was assigned to the 100th Air Division.

October 1   Northrop's Bruce Hinds and Col. Rick Couch received the Society of Experimental Test Pilots' Iven C. Kincheloe Award for outstanding performance in flight testing.

October 19   B-2A number two (82-1067), or AV-2, successfully completed its first flight. It flew from Palmdale to Edwards AFB and was heavily instrumented. The flight lasted 2 hr and 36 min. It was flown by Northrop's Leroy Schroeder and Lt. Col. John Small of the 6510th Test Squadron at Edwards. It later served as the loads test aircraft, in addition to performance and weapons carriage testing and further envelope expansion.

October 23   B-2 number one made its seventeenth flight, which lasted 5 hr and 19 min. It was flown by Northrop's Bruce Hinds and Lt. Col. Tom LeBeau, the chief operational test and evaluation (OT&E) pilot assigned to the B-2 CTF.

November 22   Exactly 2 years after its rollout, according to the USAF, B-2 number one had logged more than 95 hours in more than 25 flights.

1991

March 30   According to the Secretary of Defense's certification, the B-2A had successfully concluded early Block 2 testing, including flying qualities and performance evaluations, without any significant technical or operational problems.

June 5   The first B-2 cross-country flight was made. B-2 number one flew from Edwards to Andrews AFB just outside Washington, DC. For what was called "Stealth Week," it was then put on display with a Lockheed F-117A stealth fighter, one of two Lockheed/Boeing/General Dynamics YF-22A Advanced Tactical Fighter prototypes and an AGM-129A advanced cruise missile.

June 18   B-2A number three, or AV-3 (82-1068), made its successful first flight, Palmdale to Edwards AFB. This aircraft was the first B-2 equipped with a full complement of avionics equipment—radar, navigation, defensive, and offensive systems.

September 1   The 509th Bomb Wing, Heavy or BW(H), was redesignated the 509th Bomb Wing, or BW.

1992

March 20   B-2 number one (AV-1), having made its first flight on July 17, 1989, completed its development test program and was subsequently placed in long-term temporary storage at Edwards AFB to await future testing and, ultimately, its upgrade to Block 30 status for delivery to the 509th BW as the twenty-first and last operational B-2. It had earlier undergone an extensive radar cross section testing program and was the initial platform for envelope expansion, night flight, and both day and night aerial refueling operations.

April 17   B-2A number four, or AV-4 (82-1069), made its first flight from Palmdale to Edwards AFB; it was used in avionics and armament testing.

May 6   The Robert J. Collier Trophy, the prestigious aviation award presented annually by the National Aeronautic Association, was presented to "the Northrop Corporation, the Industry Team, and the United States Air Force for the design, development, production, and flight testing of the B-2 aircraft, which has contributed significantly to America's enduring leadership in aerospace and the country's future national security."

June 2   The USAF Strategic Air Command (SAC), activated on March 21, 1946, was deactivated. Simultaneously, SAC, and the 509th BW, became entities of the newly activated USAF Air Combat Command (ACC).

June 4   The first B-2 nighttime flight was made.

July 2   The first B-2 nighttime aerial refueling flight was made.

September 3   The first B-2 bomb (inert) drop test was successfully demonstrated at an Edwards AFB bomb range.

October 5   B-2A number five, or AV-5 (82-1070), completed its first flight from Palmdale to Edwards AFB. It was used in armament, climatic, and low-observable test phases.

1993

February 2   B-2A number six, or AV-6 (82-1071), the sixth and final full-scale development, or FSD, B-2 aircraft, made its first flight from Palmdale to Edwards AFB. It was used for technical order validation, weapons, and avionics testing. (*Author's note:* FSD is now known as engineering and manufacturing development, or EMD.)

March 1 to 5   The most B-2 flights in one week were recorded—eight.

April 1   The 509th BW returned to operational status when Brig. Gen. (Select) Ronald C. Marcotte accepted command of the wing. The initial cadre came from Detachment 509, 351st Missile Wing (MW), which was simultaneously deactivated.

July 1   The 509th BW accepted host unit duties for Whiteman AFB from the 351st MW.

July 20   The first aircraft to be assigned to the 509th BW in almost three years—a Northrop T-38 Talon (62-0609)—touched down at Whiteman AFB; it was flown in by 509th BW commander Brig. Gen. Marcotte.

September 22   The first planned operational B-2A (88-0329), called ACC-1, made its first flight at Palmdale; a 2-hr, 50-min test hop culminating at Edwards AFB.

October 13   A B-2A made the longest flight to date: 9 hr and 12 min.

December 17   After its flight from Edwards AFB, the first operational B-2A (88-0329) was delivered in a ceremony to the 509th BW at Whiteman AFB. Flown by ACC commander Gen. Michael Loh and copiloted by Lt. Col. John Bellanger, it arrived shortly after 2:00 p.m. local time. Historically, it was the 90th anniversary of the Wright Brother's first flight, and the 49th anniversary of the 509th BW.

December 22   As an operational aircraft, the first B-2A sortie was generated from Whiteman AFB.

December 31 A B-2A (AV-5 or 82-1070) successfully completed a rigorous six-month program at the Climatic Testing Laboratory at Eglin AFB, Florida.

1994

January 24 The 509th BW's Operation Group's Loading Standardization Crew and the
393rd Bomb Squadron (BS) Lead Crew successfully completed the first bomb loading
exercise on the 509th's first B-2A.

March 1 As of this date, the six FSD (now EMD) B-2s had logged more than 1,600 hours in
more than 340 flights.

March 31 In a ceremony held at Northrop's Site 4 B-2A Final Assembly Facility at Palmdale, the USAF bestowed the fleet name of *Spirit* on the B-2A aircraft. Simultaneously,
the first operational B-2A (88-0329) was named the Spirit of MISSOURI.

May 16 As a part of ACC's Power Projection Day, the Spirit of MISSOURI flew to Andrews
AFB, Maryland, where it was displayed alongside of a Lockheed F-117A Nighthawk—the
world's first operational stealth aircraft—as well as some other stealthy air vehicles. This
event marked the first time an operational B-2A Spirit had landed outside of Whiteman
AFB.

May 16 to 21 The Spirit of MISSOURI (88-0329) flew five sorties in six days, the first time
any B-2A had flown that many flights in such a short time period. In all, the MISSOURI
logged 14.6 flying hours during this six-day time span.

June The Northrop Corporation completed its acquisition of the Grumman Corporation,
thereby forming the Northrop Grumman Corporation. In 1994, Northrop Grumman
completed its acquisition of Vought Aircraft. Thus, the Northrop B-2A Spirit became the
Northrop Grumman B-2A Spirit.

August 17 The second operational B-2A (88-0330), named the Spirit of CALIFORNIA,
arrived at Whiteman AFB.

August 31 The third operational B-2A (88-0328), the Spirit of TEXAS, arrived at Whiteman
AFB.

September 23 The second operational B-2A (the Spirit of CALIFORNIA) carried out the
first-ever operational delivery of munitions by a B-2A when it flew to the Utah Test and
Training Range (UTTR) and dropped two 2,000-lb inert Mk 84 conventional bombs.

October 29 The fourth operational B-2A (88-0332), named the Spirit of WASHINGTON on
the following day, arrived at Whiteman AFB.

November 4 Defense Secretary William Perry said he firmly opposes renewing production of the B-2: "I'm not going to support a B-2 restart. I don't have the last word on everything that happens in this town [Washington, DC], but I have a pretty big word on that
issue."

November 29 Northrop Grumman offered to sell the USAF 20 additional B-2A Spirit
bombers for a fixed price of $11.4 billion, or for an average cost of $570 million each, the
last of which would be delivered the year 2003.

December 17 The 509th BW, first formed as the 509th Composite Group (CG), celebrated
its 50th anniversary.

December 30 The fifth operational B-2A (88-0331), the Spirit of SOUTH CAROLINA,
arrived at Whiteman AFB. With this delivery, in just one year the 509th BW had received
a total of four combat-ready B-2As for a grand total of five.

December 31   To date, six EMD (formerly FSD) B-2 flight-test air vehicles had logged more than 2,300 hours in more than 490 flights; thus, approximately 50 percent of the planned flight-test hours had been completed.

1995

January 12   Starting at 1:37 p.m. local time, the 509th BW launched three B-2As within 35 minutes of each other, marking the first time that three Spirits were in the sky at the same time. Each of the three aircraft completed aerial refuelings, simulated bomb runs, and transitions (landings, rearming, and takeoffs) for a record total of six B-2A sorties in a single day.

January 23   An undisclosed number of B-2As made their first appearance at the USAF's periodic Red Flag exercise held at Nellis AFB, Nevada. The aircraft participated in that Red Flag exercise through February 15.

February 17   The 509th BW's sixth operational B-2A (89-0127), the Spirit of KANSAS, arrived at Whiteman AFB.

June 10 to 11   Piloted by 509th BW commander Brig. Gen. Marcotte, the Spirit of MISSOURI (88-0329) flew nonstop from Whiteman AFB to Paris, France, to participate in a flyover at the internationally famous Paris Air Show. The aircraft then landed, and for about one hour, its engines still running, flight crews were changed for its return flight to Missouri. To date, the 11-hr-plus flight to Paris, and the 13-hr-plus flight back to Whiteman AFB, marked the longest flights ever recorded by the B-2A fleet.

June 28   The seventh operational B-2A (89-0128), named the Spirit of NEBRASKA, arrived at Whiteman AFB.

September 1   The Spirit of KANSAS (89-0127), the sixth operational B-2A, flew to Honolulu, Hawaii, to take part in the next day's 50th anniversary celebration of America's victory in the Pacific theater during World War II. The trip marked the Spirit's first mission over the Pacific Ocean.

September 3   The seventh operational B-2A, which had arrived at Whiteman AFB earlier on June 28, was named the Spirit of NEBRASKA during a ceremony at Offutt AFB, Nebraska—the former home of the USAF's Strategic Air Command (deactivated on 2 June 1992). Whiteman AFB personnel welcomed home the NEBRASKA on the same day while dedicating two of the 509th BW's T-38 Talons, the Spirit of Sedalia and Spirit of Warrensburg, in honor of the base's two neighboring communities.

November 9   The first operational B-2A, the Spirit of MISSOURI (88-0329), was returned to Northrop Grumman's Palmdale, California, facility to undergo upgrading to Block 30 status.

November 14   The eighth operational B-2A (89-0129), named the Spirit of GEORGIA, arrived at Whiteman AFB from the Northrop Grumman plant in Palmdale, California.

December 11   Whiteman AFB welcomed back the eighth operational B-2A, the Spirit of GEORGIA, after its naming ceremony at Robins AFB, Georgia. Meanwhile, the Spirit of CALIFORNIA (88-0330)—the second operational B-2A—piloted by 509th BW commander Brig. Gen. Marcotte, escorted the newly named GEORGIA back to Whiteman from Robins, thereby marking the 509th sortie flown by the 509th BW's growing fleet of B-2As; three having been delivered during the year 1995.

1996

January 10   The ninth operational B-2A (90-0041), named the Spirit of HAWAII, arrived at Whiteman AFB.

January 24   The 509th BW reached a major milestone when the tenth operational B-2A (90-0040), the Spirit of ALASKA, arrived at Whiteman AFB.

February 8   Two B-2As, the Spirit of CALIFORNIA (88-0330) and Spirit of WASHINGTON (88-0332), departed Whiteman for a flight to Andersen AFB, Guam, as part of the ACC's Global Power mission activities and to participate in the 1996 Asian Aerospace Air Show. Both aircraft arrived back at Whiteman on February 11.

March 10   The Spirit of WASHINGTON (88-0332) made a flyover appearance at the FIDAE 1996 Air Show in Santiago, Chile, after which it returned to Whiteman. The 24.5-hr flight was the longest B-2A Global Power mission.

April 30   The Tacit Blue (Whale) was announced by the USAF as one of its most successful technology demonstration programs; it had made its first flight in February 1982 and logged another 134 flights afterwards. The aircraft provided valuable engineering data and validated innovative stealth technology advances that aided in the B-2 design, as well as other platforms.

May 15   The 11th operational B-2A (93-1085), the Spirit of OKLAHOMA, arrived at Whiteman AFB. This event marked yet another significant milestone in the B-2 program, because this was the first Block 20 aircraft to arrive.

May 21   A B-2 precautionary stand-down ended. The 509th BW's B-2 bomber fleet was under a precautionary stand-down that began on May 10, because of concerns regarding a clamp in the aircraft's tailpipe assembly. Each B-2 has eight tailpipe clamps, two on each engine. The problem was corrected.

Mid-1996   B-2A number five (82-1070) successfully completed cold-climate testing at Eielson AFB Alaska.

May 22   Tacit Blue (Whale) was publicly unveiled at the U.S. Air Force Museum. This was the first opportunity for the public to see the aircraft.

June 1   The 509th BW flew its first Block 20 sortie with its eleventh operational B-2A (93-1085), the Spirit of OKLAHOMA.

July 3   The twelfth operational B-2A (92-0700), named the Spirit of FLORIDA, arrived at Whiteman AFB; it being the second Block 20 aircraft.

July 12   The 509th BW received its first combat-ready GATS/GAM 2,000-lb near-precision conventional weapons.

August 30   To be later named the Spirit of KITTY HAWK, the thirteenth operational B-2A (93-1086) arrived at Whiteman AFB.

October 8   Three B-2As successfully executed the first live drops of Global Positioning (Satellite) System-Aided Munition (GAM) conventional weapons at a test range on Nellis AFB, Nevada. In all, the trio of Spirits dropped 16 of the unique munitions against 16 different targets from altitudes of about 40,000 ft and down-range distances of more than 6 mi. All 16 targets were destroyed. Also during the exercise, Maj. Rex Bailey became the first USAF pilot to log 500 hours in B-2A aircraft.

October 23   The twelfth operational B-2A (92-0700), having arrived at Whiteman AFB on July 3, was named the Spirit of FLORIDA in a naming ceremony at MacDill AFB, Florida.

November 7   Headquarters ACC activated the 394th Combat Training Squadron (CTS) at Whiteman AFB and assigned the new unit to the 509th BW.

November 11   Captains Scott Vander Hamm and Scott Hughes completed a 38-hr long-endurance B-2A simulator flight, possibly the longest simulator flight to date in USAF history.

November 21   Flown by Col. James Macon, 509th BW Vice Wing commander, and Maj. Len Litton, the Spirit of WASHINGTON (88-0332) recorded the 509th BW's one-thousandth B-2A flight; this total averaged 1.1 flights per day since December 17, 1993.

December 17   On the 52nd anniversary of the 509th BW, the thirteenth operational B-2A (93-1086) was named the Spirit of KITTY HAWK during a naming ceremony at Seymour Johnson AFB, North Carolina. The 509th BW had received another five B-2As during the year 1996, bringing the total to six for the year.

1997

January 1   The USAF announced an early *limited* initial operational capability (IOC) for the B-2A Spirit. It added that the 509th BW's fleet of 13 operational B-2A aircraft had become available for use in the conventional, as well as the nuclear, bombardment role.

January 21 to 27   A 31-member team from the ACC Inspector General (IG) Office conducted a Nuclear Security Inspection of the 509th BW.

February 7   Maj. Steven Moulton and Capt. Jeff Long completed a record-setting 44.4-hr long-endurance B-2A simulator flight.

February 19   The 509th BW conducted a generation exercise that included the first-ever B-2A aircraft taxi exercise in response to an Exercise Emergency Action Message, or EEAM.

March 6 to 7   Gen. Ronald R. Fogelman, Air Force chief of staff, visited Whiteman AFB, during which he attended the 509th BW's Initial Operational Capability Dining-Out, held on March 6.

April 1   The USAF announced *full* initial operational capability (IOC) for the 509th BW's fleet of 13 operational B-2As.

June   After some eight years and nearly 1,000 missions, the flight-test program for the B-2 stealth bomber was completed; in all, seven B-2s participated in the long-running test program.

July 6 to 7   The Spirit of NEBRASKA (89-0128), crewed by Majs. Chris Inman and Steve Moulton, departed from Whiteman AFB at 8:07 a.m. local time on July 6. The aircraft and crew returned to Whiteman at 9:43 a.m. local time on July 7 after a 14,414-mi flight to Guam and back.

July 18   Named the Spirit of OHIO, the fourteenth operational B-2A (82-1070) arrived at Whiteman AFB.

August 5   To be later named the Spirit of PENNSYLVANIA, the fifteenth operational B-2A (93-1087) arrived at Whiteman AFB.

August 6   As part of the START treaty agreement between the American and Russian governments, eight of nine operational B-2As at Whiteman were put on display in response to an open-display request from Russia. Six of the 509th BW's B-2As had been returned to Palmdale for their respective modifications to Block 30 standard.

August 7   The fifteenth operational B-2A, the first Block 30 B-2A (93-1087), was named the Spirit of PENNSYLVANIA in a ceremony at Willow Grove Reserve Air Station, near Philadelphia. Capt. Scott Vander Hamm of the 394th Combat Training Squadron (CTS) and Lt. Col. Tom Cressman from the Palmdale test team piloted AV-20 from Palmdale to

Willow Grove. It soon departed for Whiteman AFB, where it was welcomed as the fifteenth named B-2A. Lt. Col. Jonathan George, 509th Operations Group deputy commander, and Maj. Steve Moulton, 394th CTS, flew to Whiteman AFB. It had arrived at Whiteman two days earlier.

October 10   Named the Spirit of NEW YORK, the sixteenth operational B-2A (82-1068) arrived at Whiteman AFB.

November 6   The Spirit of PENNSYLVANIA (93-1087) participated in a special test when it dropped several inert Joint Direct Attack Munitions, or JDAMs, during a flight over the Utah Test Range. During a different mission, the Spirit of FLORIDA (92-0700), having been outfitted with a new bomb rack assembly (BRA), flew a test mission. The new BRA allows the B-2A to carry an even larger assortment of munitions into combat.

November 10   Named the Spirit of LOUISIANA, the seventeenth operational B-2A (93-1088) arrived at Whitman AFB. It was also the second Block 30 B-2 to join the fleet.

December 4   Unnamed at the time, the third Block 30 B-2 recently arrived at Whiteman as reported in a 509th BW Public Affairs Office news release on this date. The airplane, called "Air Vehicle 2," formerly served as FSD B-2 number two.

1998

January 8   The 325th Bomb Squadron (BS) was activated at Whiteman AFB and assigned to the 509th BW. The new unit became the 509th BW's second operational bomb squadron.

February 26   Eight members of President Clinton's Long-Range Air Power Panel visited Whiteman AFB. The nine-member panel is studying the need for future long-range bombers and the appropriate number of B-2A stealth bombers needed to fulfill that mission.

March 17   A B-2 dropped two B61-11 bombshells (casings) to test their improved ground-penetration capability at the Stuart Creek Impact Area, 35 mi southeast of Fairbanks, Alaska. The tests were designed to measure the nuclear bomb casing's penetration into frozen soil and the survivability of the weapon's internal components. These were the final two tests needed to certify the weapon system as operational. This new case design lets this nuclear device penetrate the ground to a depth of 15 to 25 ft, where it would then detonate.

March 17   Two Russian military officers met with senior Whiteman AFB leaders and received a B-2 program orientation. The two visited as part of the Defense Department's continuing military-to-military visits sponsored under the 1992 Nunn-Lugar Cooperative Threat Reduction Program. The program increases stability by fostering trust and understanding between the United States and Russia.

March 20   The USAF named the eighteenth operational B-2A the Spirit of ARIZONA in a ceremony at Davis-Monthan AFB, Arizona. After the ceremony, the ARIZONA was delivered to Whiteman AFB on the same day.

March 20 to 22   Approximately 250 509th BW personnel are deployed to Andersen AFB, Guam, via C-5B Galaxy cargo aircraft as part of Island Spirit, a 10-day Global Power exercise.

March 23   The Spirit of LOUISIANA (93-1088), crewed by Brig. Gen. Tom Goslin Jr., commander of the 509th BW, and Maj. Jim Schmidt, and the Spirit of PENNSYLVANIA (93-1087), flown by Captains Tony Monetti and Christopher Harness, left Whiteman AFB for

Andersen AFB, Guam, as part of the Island Spirit exercise. Both aircraft returned on April 5, while the deployed 509th BW personnel arrived home during the week of April 12.

March 30 The Spirit of PENNSYLVANIA (93-1087), crewed by Captains Tony Monetti and Christopher Harness, dropped the first operational maximum load of Mk-82 500-lb bombs. The 40,000-plus lb of live conventional weapons were targeted against a tiny island in the Farralon Range in the Pacific Ocean.

April 9 After a lengthy competition with Boeing, Lockheed Martin won the right to develop and produce the next generation of stealthy, air-launched cruise missiles. Known as the AGM-158A Joint Air-to-Surface Standoff Missile, or JASSAM, the new weapons will have a range of 115 nmi. Slated for use by the B-2A and others, at this writing, the USAF wants to procure 2,400 of the satellite-guided weapons.

April 10 It was announced that small holes had been discovered in one of the operational B-2A aircraft. "The damage could cost up to $500 thousand to repair," the USAF said. The cause of the damage was unknown at the time, "but it may have been the result of a lightning strike at Whiteman AFB," the USAF added.

April 28 The 509th BW completed another first when it successfully dropped several of the newly developed deep-penetration Joint Direct Attack Munition, or JDAM, based upon the BLU-109. The test involved releasing four of the 2,000-lb class weapons on a White Sands, New Mexico, test range against deeply buried targets.

May 23 Named the Spirit of MISSISSIPPI, the nineteenth operational B-2A (82-1071)—formerly the sixth FSD air vehicle, arrived at Whiteman AFB.

June Brig. Gen. Leroy Barnidge Jr. became commander of the 509th BW, succeeding Brig. Gen. Thomas Goslin Jr.

June 10 The 509th BW began its first-ever operational readiness inspection or ORI on this date. It was a 12-day, around-the-clock inspection, which in conclusion completely satisfied the inspection teams from Air Combat Command, the Defense Special Weapons Agency, Air Force Safety Center, U.S. Strategic Command, and U.S. Atlantic Command.

July Col. Don Higgins Jr. becomes vice commander of the 509th BW, succeeding Col. Dave Shunk.

August 6 The 509th BW commander suspended peacetime training missions for the B-2. The precautionary stand-down was the result of a potential problem associated with initiators that operate the aircrew ejection system.

September 4 For what the DoD—actually, the Joint Chiefs of Staff—called 30 days of "training operations," three B-2As were quickly deployed to Guam. The B-2's mission, according to a senior USAF officer, was to "fly some fairly long, highly visible missions throughout the theater." They were accompanied by three Barksdale AFB, Louisiana, B-52Hs.

October 6 Lt. Gen. Ronald C. Marcotte, 8th Air Force commander and the first 509th BW commander, visited Whiteman AFB. As commander of the legendary 8th AF, he oversees the war-fighting capability of not only the B-2A Spirit, but the B-1B, B-52H, F-15, F-16, and A-10 aircraft. Whiteman AFB is one of seven air bases assigned to the 8th Air Force.

November 14 As an undisclosed number of Whiteman AFB-based B-2s prepared to participate in Operation Desert Thunder, Iraq once more backed down from an imminent attack for refusing to let United Nations weapons inspectors perform their duties. If the operation had proceeded, it would have been the B-2's combat debut.

November 22   The tenth anniversary of the rollout of the first B-2 (82-1066) at USAF Plant 42, Site 4, Palmdale, California was celebrated.

December 16   U.S. military forces launched a "strong, sustained series of air strikes" against Iraq shortly after 5:00 p.m., Washington DC time. The 509th BW was, of course, put on alert for possible action in what was called Operation Desert Fox. The operation lasted four days, and no B-2s were used.

December 17   The fifth anniversary of the arrival of the 509th BW's first B-2—the Spirit of MISSOURI.

1999

March 24 to 25   Two unidentified B-2As and their crews, after flying nonstop from Whiteman AFB, successfully dropped 32 GBU-31 2,000-lb (900-kg) class JDAM weapons on independently targeted facilities in the former Republic of Yugoslavia as they participated in their very first combat missions as part of NATO's Operation Allied Force and the Defense Department's Operation Noble Anvil. The two B-2s took off in the early morning hours on March 24 (local time) and returned to Whiteman some 31 hours later.

March 25 to 26   Another two unidentified B-2s and crews flew a second nonstop mission to bomb Serbian targets.

March 29   It was announced that the B-2 Spirit had met every expectation since the type's operational debut on March 24.

April 1   The USAF announced it wanted to procure more Boeing guidance kits for 2,000-lb satellite-guided smart bombs and accelerate the production of items under contract. B-2s had dropped 224 of the GBU-31 JDAMs during NATO's first seven days of air strikes against Yugoslavia. The weapon can be launched in all weather and land as close as 30 ft from its programmed coordinates. The Pentagon has requested $126 million in the fiscal 2000 defense budget to buy 5,410 guidance kits that will convert the unguided Mk-84/BLU-109 2,000-lb bombs into guided ones. The kits are manufactured at Boeing's Aircraft and Systems Group facility in St. Charles, Missouri. That's up from 1,782 kits ordered in fiscal 1999.

April 5   Twelve days into NATO's Operation Allied Force, a total of 384 JDAMs had been launched by B-2s from the 509th BW. That is, two aircraft and 32 GBU-31s were used each day. No B-2s or B-2 crews of Operation Allied Force had been identified at this time.

April 8   The 509th BW had flown at least a dozen missions by this date; 384 JDAMs launched.

April 12   On day 20 of Operation Allied Force, without any B-2 aircraft or crew identification thus far, the USAF—in particular, the ACC—continued to rave about the good job the 509th BW was doing.

April 13   In an e-mailed message to this writer, Senior Airman Pauline Gates of the 509th BW Public Affairs Office wrote: "I still can't give you names of crews. We only have eight B-2s on station. As for missions, I can say we have flown more than a dozen missions. Two planes each, 16 JDAMs each. That's the best I can do."

May 22   The twentieth operational B-2 (82-1069), formerly FSD B-2 number four, was named the Spirit of INDIANA.

June 1   By this date, the 509th BW had flown more than 40 missions and had launched more than 1,280 GBU-31 JDAMs in Operation Allied Force.

July 17   The tenth anniversary of the first flight of B-2 number one—Palmdale to Edwards AFB.

2000

Early 2000   To be named the Spirit of AMERICA (pending), the twenty-first and last operational B-2A is to be delivered to the 509th BW. Ironically, the twenty-first and last operational B-2A is the very first one to be built.

2003

December 17   The tenth anniversary of the first B-2 delivery to the 509th BW at Whiteman AFB is to be celebrated.

2014

July 17   The twenty-fifth anniversary of the B-2's first flight is to be celebrated.

ACC	Air Combat Command
ACDS	Adaptive Control Drilling System
ACES II	Advanced Concept Ejection Seat II
ACM	Advanced Cruise Missile
AEF	Air Expeditionary Force
AEG/W	Air Expeditionary Group/Wing
AFB	Air Force Base
AFFTC	Air Force Flight Test Center
AFMC	Air Force Material Command
AFSC	Air Force Systems Center
AGM	Air-to-Ground Missile
ALCM	Air-Launched Cruise Missile
AMSA	Advanced Manned Strategic Aircraft
ARPA	Advanced Research Projects Agency
ATA	Advanced Technology Aircraft
ATB	Advanced Technology Bomber
ATR	Automatic Target Recognition
BDA	Bomb Damage Assessment
BG	Bombardment Group
BRA	Bomb Rack Assembly
BW	Bomb Wing
CAD/CAM	Computer-Aided Design/Computer-Aided Manufacturing
CALCM	Conventional (Warhead) Air-Launched Cruise Missile
CEP	Circular Error Probable
CTS	Combat Training Squadron
GBU	Guided Bomb Unit
GLAS	Gust Load Alleviation System
GPS	Global Positioning System
HARM	High-Speed Antiradiation Missile
JASSM	Joint Air-to-Surface Standoff Missile
JDAM	Joint Direct Attack Munition

JSOW	Joint Standoff Weapon
JV 2010	Joint Vision 2010
LPI	Low Probability of Intercept
LRCA	Long-Range Combat Aircraft
MX	Materiel, Experimental
OTH	Over-the-Horizon
PGM	Precision-Guided Munition
RAM	Radar-Absorbing Material
RAS	Radar-Absorbing Structure
RCS	Radar Cross Section
SAC	Strategic Air Command
SAM	Surface-to-Air Missile
SAR	Synthetic Aperture Radar
SFW	Sensor-Fused Weapon
SIOP	Single Integrated Operational Plan
SRAM	Short-Range Attack Missile
SWL	Strategic Weapons Launcher
TERCOM	Terrain Contour Matching
TSSAM	Tri-Service Standoff Attack Missile
UAV	Unmanned Aerial Vehicle
WS	Weapon System

Air Force magazine, published monthly by the Air Force Association, Arlington, Virginia; various issues from January 1988.

Aviation Week and Space Technology magazine, published weekly by McGraw-Hill, New York; various issues since January 1980.

Coleman, Ted, with Robert Wenkam. *Jack Northrop and the Flying Wing: The Story Behind The Stealth Bomber.* New York: Paragon House, 1988.

Goodall, James C. *America's Stealth Fighters and Bombers.* Osceola, Wis.: MBI Publishing Co., 1992.

Janes All the World's Aircraft. McGraw-Hill, New York, 1990 to 1991 and on.

Lear, Tom. *Historical Look at Northrop Corporation. Aerotech News and Review* magazine, published weekly by AEROTECH; Souvenir Edition, Volume 4, No. 22, August 11, 1989.

Air Force Report Details Capabilities of B-2. Aerotech News and Review magazine, published weekly by AEROTECH; Souvenir Edition, Volume 4, No. 22, August 11, 1989.

Miller, Jay. *Northrop Grumman B-2A Spirit.* Arlington, Tex.: Aerofax, Inc., 1991.

Mizrahi, Joseph V. "Sizing Up Stealth." *Wings* magazine, Granada Hills, California, February 1990.

Pace, Steve. *Lockheed Skunk Works.* Osceola, Wisconsin: Motorbooks International, 1992.

——. *X-Fighters: USAF Experimental and Prototype Fighters, XP-59 to YF-23.* Osceola, Wisconsin: Motorbooks International, 1991.

Rich, Ben R. and Janos, Leo. *Skunk Works.* New York: Little, Brown and Co., 1994.

Scott, Bill. *Inside the Stealth Bomber: the B-2 Story.* New York: TAB/AERO Books, a division of McGraw-Hill, Inc., 1991.

Spitzer, Paul. *Flying Wing: What's New Is Old; What's Old Is New. Boeing News,* published weekly by Boeing; Volume 48, No. 6, February 10, 1989.

Sweetman, Bill. *Aurora: The Pentagon's Secret Hypersonic Spyplane.* Osceola, Wis.: Motorbooks International, 1993.

Steve Pace is a veteran aviation journalist and author who has written 17 books on a wide range of military aircraft and related topics. He lives in Tacoma, Washington.